AUGUSTINE

AUGUSTINE

MAJOR WRITINGS

═══ ✦ ═══

Benedict J. Groeschel, C.F.R.

CROSSROAD • NEW YORK

This Printing: 2007

The Crossroad Publishing Company
16 Penn Plaza, 481 Eighth Avenue, New York, NY 10001

Printed in the United States of America

The author acknowledges with gratitude the permission of the following
publishers to use copyrighted material, the source of which is indicated in the
text: Augustinian Press for *We Are Your Servants;* University of California Press
for *Augustine of Hippo* by Peter Brown; Catholic University of America Press for
The City of God and selections from *Fathers of the Church;* Paulist Press for
Augustine of Hippo by Mary T. Clark and selections from *Ancient Christian
Writers;* International Commission on English in the Liturgy for several quota-
tions from *The Liturgy of the Hours;* New City Press for *The Works of St.
Augustine,* translated by Edmund Hill; Sheed & Ward for *The Confessions of St.
Augustine,* translated by Frank Sheed.

Library of Congress Cataloging-in-Publication Data

Groeschel, Benedict J.
    Augustine : Major writings / Benedict J.
Groeschel.
        p.   cm. — (The Crossroad spiritual legacy series)
    Includes bibliographical references.
    ISBN 0-8245-2505-1
    1. Augustine, Saint, Bishop of Hippo. I. Augustine, Saint,
Bishop of Hippo. Selections. English. 1995. II. Title.
III. Series
BR65.A9G77   1995
270.2'092—dc20
    [B]   95-3453
                                                            CIP

Dedication

To St. Augustine,
my teacher,

and to St. Francis,
my father,

whose life echoed so much
of what Augustine taught.

Cover Art: *St. Augustine,* by John Lynch. "What is that light that shines upon me and strikes me and strikes at my heart with no wounding? . : . It is Wisdom itself which in these moments shines upon me, cleaving through my cloud."

(*Confessions* 11.9)

Contents

Foreword

Writing in the fourth century, a North African Christian by the name of Lactantius offered the following definition of virtue. For him, virtue is nothing less than "enduring of evils and labors." How unlike contemporary notions this definition of virtue is and how odd it sounds for us to be told so plainly that the fullness of life can be had only through enduring evils and trials. Yet, despite our inclination to write off Lactantius as an overly pessimistic nay-sayer, we must admit that life does include a large dose of suffering. We can take it well or badly. We can flee it or embrace it, but it will come and find us wherever we hide, and then it will test our mettle. Virtue does involve suffering evils, not simply actualizing ourselves, or conquering our fears, or visualizing success, or learning techniques to cope with stress, or building better "relationships" with members of the opposite sex. There are things in life that simply cannot be so easily manipulated. Situations that don't get better. Unpleasant realities that won't go away. Where do we turn when confronted by them?

We can turn to the externals, to our comforts and our conveniences, to the superficialities of our lives, or we can turn to our depths. Many who have lived before us have learned the hard way that turning to the depths is the way to a fuller life. Their insights have been handed down, often in forms that are now hard to find and harder to read. Their language is archaic. Their morality out of sync with ours. Their clarity, off-putting. Their humility, disconcerting. Yet they are there, waiting quietly to share with us their hard-won wisdom, waiting to dialogue with us as we face situations that are different from those they encountered only in the particulars, not in the essences.

Simply put, that is the reason why Crossroad, myself, and a team of well-known scholars and spiritual leaders have joined together to undertake the Spiritual Legacy series. The need for spiritual wisdom is great. Our situation is critical. This, then, is more than an enterprise in scholarship, more than a literary exercise. It is an effort to convey life.

Certainly the idea of doing editions of the works of spiritual guides from the past is not new. There are a host of books available that do just that. How is the Spiritual Legacy series different?

The uniqueness of this series abides in its content and its style. In content it endeavors to present both texts from the spiritual guide and extensive commentary by a present-day disciple of the sage. It gives the reader the chance to encounter for herself the writings of a spiritual master. Nothing can take the place of that experience. However demanding it might be, whatever efforts it might require, there can be no substitute for it. One, for instance, cannot simply hear a description of the tenth chapter of Augustine's *Confessions*. No commentary, however skilled, can take the place of reading for oneself Augustine's words of unparalleled power: "Late have I loved Thee, O Beauty, so ancient, yet so new!"

While it is true that there is no substitute for encountering the text firsthand, it is also certain that for most people that encounter will be an excursion into a foreign land. Often many centuries and numerous barriers of language, customs, philosophy, and style separate us from the writings of bygone sages. To come to that point where we can understand the horizon of the author, we must be taught something about the historical context, the literary style, and the thought forms of the age, for instance. That is why we have included in this series extensive commentary on the text. That commentary is alternated with the text throughout the books, so that one can be taught, then experience the writings firsthand, over and over as one moves deeper into the text. At that point, the horizon of the reader meets that of the author, aided by the expert guidance of the editor of each book, who suggests not only what the text might mean, but how it might be made part of our lives.

The style of the Spiritual Legacy series is also unique in that it attempts to convey life with a certain degree of sophistication that befits an educated readership. Yet it does not assume that everyone will have a background in the material presented, nor does it purport to offer original or arcane scholarship. The editors' mastery of the texts is in each case complemented by their experience in putting the meaning of the texts into practice and helping others to do so as well. We are trying to present a series of books that will fit somewhere between the scholarly editions that pride themselves on their accuracy and originality and the popular pieces that offer too little substance for the healthy reader.

The series is designed to be used by a broad range of people. For those seekers who wish to journey toward spiritual wholeness as part of a group, the series is ideally suited. The texts presented can be easily divided into sections for discussion by a group meeting, say, on a weekly basis.

For those who are traveling alone, the series is a trustworthy and enjoyable tour book. The direct, simple language of the commentaries frames the memorable words of the classical texts and offers them in an attractive setting for meditation and practical application.

The publisher and editors of the Spiritual Legacy series join me in inviting you to undertake a journey that will take you back to an encounter with ancient wisdom and challenge you to an experience of self-understanding and, at its best, self-transcendence. It is our hope that that experience will help you to grow and to be a source of fresh life for all those around you.

John Farina

Acknowledgments

I am deeply grateful to John Farina for inviting me to do this volume because it has given me the opportunity to make some return to St. Augustine for all that he has taught me for almost half a century. John, along with Bob Heller of Crossroad, has patiently prodded me along as I worked on the great corpus of Augustine's writings. Invaluable assistance was provided generously by two outstanding sons of St. Augustine; Fr. John Rotelle, O.S.A., and Fr. Allan Fitzgerald, O.S.A., both members of the Augustinian family at Villanova. I have in this text acknowledged various scholars and translators whose works have guided me along the way, but I must mention especially Sr. Mary Clark, R.S.C.J., Fr. Edmund Hill, O.P., and Dr. Bernard McGinn, although none of them had any responsibility for what I have written.

The remarkable symbolic portrait of St. Augustine on the book cover was provided by a young artist, John Lynch, who, while studying for the priesthood, has done several covers for my books. I am grateful to him and to Ann Cicchelli, who has so patiently and professionally typed the manuscript in several revisions. I need to thank Deacon Bob Esposito and Michael Sarro for their generous use of time. Thanks go to Brother Clement, O.S.B., and Brother Meinrad, O.S.B., of Prince of Peace Abbey in Oceanside, California, and to David Burns and Charles Szivos of St. Joseph's Seminary in Yonkers, New York, for checking the manuscript. I also wish to express my sincere gratitude to the cloistered religious, nuns and monks, as well as several devout lay people who pray fervently for my works and who keep me going by their loving concern, and finally to the friars and sisters of the Franciscans of the Renewal, who patiently endure having writers in their midst.

Fr. Benedict Joseph Groeschel, C.F.R.
St. Crispin Friary
Bronx, New York

Feast of the Immaculate Conception, 1994

Introduction

When I was asked to write this book introducing readers to St. Augustine as a spiritual writer, my first impulse was to defer in favor of any one of several Augustinian scholars who have spent their lives mining the gold of his thought. However, the publishers of this series explained that they wanted a book for those who are only slightly familiar with Augustine and who would approach the immense corpus of his work looking for "spiritual reading." I felt a bit more assured because without exaggeration I can say that I have read something from St. Augustine almost every day for the past forty-five years.

While St. Francis is my father, St. Augustine has been my guide more than anyone else in studying the Scriptures, in attempts at daily conversion, and even in the study of human behavior and spiritual guidance. Despite the press of duties, I accepted this task because of my debt to this great saint and because I knew that there were Augustinian scholars whom I could rely on either personally or through their works. In this book I will undertake to welcome those less familiar than myself to the Christian worldview of St. Augustine and to the immense riches left by this convert monk and bishop whose writings have profoundly influenced directly or indirectly the thinking of every generation since his own.

A Daunting Task

The extant writings of St. Augustine include over five million words in Latin. His impact on dogmatic and moral theology, Scripture, philosophy, history, and psychology have produced a corpus of commentaries and writings that is many times larger. When I visited the Augustinian Heritage Institute adjacent to Villanova University and encountered the volume of books available, I almost regretted my decision to write this introduction. Then when the director, Fr. John Rotelle, O.S.A., allowed me to delve into the vast storehouse of books available in English on Augustine as a spiritual writer, I felt like a man beginning to write a guidebook of the Swiss Alps. Father Allan Fitzgerald, O.S.A., spent an hour with me demonstrating his computer and his deceptively compact little box containing all of Augustine's five million words. I realized that I had to step back for a moment to catch my breath and reassure myself that I am only a devoted reader of Augustine trying to introduce other readers to these immense treasures. With all that is written if I were to write anything too original it would most certainly be foolish. I suspect that Augustine from his place in eternity (if he now cares about these things at all) is not unfamiliar with being the subject of original interpretations or attacks that are quite off the mark. However, I trust that as an old teacher he is not displeased with my modest attempt to make his thoughts available to other potential students.

The Incredible Mountains

This all leads to an invitation to a wonderful adventure in spiritual exploration. As your guide I will try to open up to you immense Augustine vistas in an orderly way, explain briefly what we are looking at from the high ledges, tell you how to explore the valleys so as to know what to read and where to find it. But beware! You may never want to leave these enchanted mountains again. After forty years I can still meditate on one book of the *Confessions* or a few sermons during a week-long retreat and come back feeling frustrated that there is still so much more gold to mine in those few pages. I, for one, know that I shall never in this life escape from the Augustinian Alps.

The first thing for us to do is to get a plan of exploration. It is very important for my fellow explorers to get a taste of the many different aspects of Augustine by sampling writings that are readily available in adequate theological libraries or from the Augustinian Heritage Foundation. It is important to proceed in an orderly way so that one is not overwhelmed. Therefore, somewhat artificially, we will consider our subject in this order: Augustine the convert, the philosopher, and psychologist; the preacher and Scripture scholar; the theologian and the historian. In every one of these categories he is also a spiritual writer. There are passages scattered through most of his works that directly relate to the spiritual journey and we have summed these up in a final chapter called "Augustine as a Spiritual Guide."

It is worth mentioning to readers unfamiliar with ancient writing (a pity in itself), that before the great medieval schoolmen, especially St. Thomas Aquinas, writers did not attempt to compose works of pure theology or pure philosophy or to restrict themselves to any one discipline when approaching a question. Philosophical ideas, quotations from Scripture and tradition and even from the classics were mixed in pellmell with personal reflections and even snatches of the writer's own experience. We are in a way familiar with such an eclectic style from more serious articles written in the popular press today. Outside of scholarly publications, writers in informed popular weeklies or monthlies often draw from several different disciplines and even from their own experience. It is necessary to keep in mind that Augustine does just that. His autobiography, the *Confessions*, contains elements and discussions of theology, philosophy, classics, psychology, apologetics, and polemics, along with fascinating vignettes of ancient Roman life and deep spiritual insights.

It is also important to recognize that we come to know authors like Augustine only through translations and that the ideas and backgrounds of the translators, however faithful they try to be, will influence our perceptions of the writer. One need only to compare an ancient English translation of the Sermon on the Mount (like the Douay or King James Version) with a completely contemporary one to realize the difference a translation may make in our responding to the original speaker, in this case our Savior.

When I was about fourteen I became entranced by one of the

few translations of the *Confessions* that was available at the time, the angular and austere work of Dr. Edward B. Pusey of the Oxford Movement.[1] I could not understand much of it and had to skip over the polemical arguments against the Manichees (I still do), but I was literally set on fire by the quotation that I had previously seen somewhere else beginning with the words "O Beauty so ancient and yet so new" (10.27).

For years St. Augustine spoke to me in Pusey's eloquent but stilted Victorian prose. Then I came to know Frank Sheed's translation, which is so much smoother but no less accurate and eloquent in its own way. Sheed's translation is much more vital and opened up to me many passages that had previously remained obscure.[2] Sheed also helpfully explained in the introduction that St. Augustine had no Latin word that is the equivalent of our stately use of the word "Thou." He could only address God through the Latin equivalent of the word "You." Later, Frank Sheed became a dear friend and shared with me this marvelous experience of a translator. Hotels in days gone by included the services of a paid typist. Frank brought several pages of his translation of the *Confessions* in longhand to a typist at a hotel where he was staying for a few days. When he picked up the manuscript the typist commented to him, "My, you have led a very interesting life."

There are now several readable translations of the *Confessions* available, and we will come to these shortly. It is interesting to compare simply this one passage in Latin and then a sample of translations to see how differently faithful scholars may interpret the same lines. Let us begin with the Latin since most of the Augustine's readers have never seen a line as he wrote it:

Sero te amavi, pulcritudo tam antiqua et tam nova, sero te amavi. Et ecce intus eras et ego foris et ibi te quaerebam et in ista formosa, quae fecisti, deformis irruebam. Mecum eras et tecum non eram. Ea me tenebant longe a te, quae si in te non essent, non essent. Vocasti et clamasti et rupisti surditatem meam, coruscasti, spenduisti et fugasti caecitatem meam; flagrasti et duxi spiritium et anhelo tibi; gustavi et esurio et sitio; tetigisti me, et exarsi in pacem tuam.

Dr. Pusey's Victorian translation follows. When you read it you will understand why it seemed to me at the time that St. Augustine was a devout Victorian gentleman, someone like Cardinal Newman.

Too late loved I Thee, O Thou Beauty of ancient days, yet ever new! Too late I loved Thee! and behold, Thou wert within, and I abroad, and there I searched for Thee; deformed I, plunging amid those fair forms, which Thou hadst made. Thou wert with me, but was not with Thee. Things held me far from Thee, which, unless they were in Thee, were not at all. Thou calledst and shoutedst burstest my deafness. Thou flashedst, shonest, and scatteredst my blindness. Thou breathedst odors, and I drew in breath and panted for Thee, I tasted and hungered and thirsted. Thou touchedst me and I burned for Thy peace.

Now we can compare Frank Sheed's translation and see that it has more color and comes closer to the way that we speak today. Sheed was convinced that Augustine's Latin was very modern for the times in which he lived. He made a concession to his English readers by keeping "Thou" in the prayer parts of his translation of the *Confessions*. In the other parts of the translation he speaks to God as "You."

Late have I loved Thee, O Beauty so ancient and so new; late have I loved Thee! For behold Thou were within me and I outside and in my unloveliness fell upon those lovely things that Thou hast made. Thou wert with me and I was not with Thee. I was kept from Thee by those things, yet had they not been in Thee, they would not have been at all. Thou didst call and cry to me and break open my deafness; and Thou didst send forth Thy beams and shine upon me and chase away my blindness; Thou didst breathe fragrance upon me, and I drew in my breath and do now pant for Thee; I tasted Thee, and now hunger and thirst for Thee; Thou didst touch me, and I have burned for Thy peace.

Sister Mary Clark, R.S.C.J., has published a superb collection of her own translations of St. Augustine along with invaluable scholarly and readable introductions in *Augustine of Hippo*.[3] Her translation has a special quality of its own—perhaps a feminine touch, which was needed since almost all previous translators were men.

Late have I loved you, O Beauty, so ancient and so new, late have I loved you! And behold, you were within me and I was outside, and there I sought for you, and in my deformity I rushed headlong into the well-formed things that you have made. You were with me, and I was not with you. Those outer beauties held me far from you, yet if they had not been in you, they would not have existed at all. You called, and cried out to me and broke open my deafness; you shone forth upon me and you scattered my blindness. You breathed fragrance, and I drew in my breath and I now pant for you. I tasted and I hunger and thirst; you touched me, and I burned for Your peace.

Though the *Confessions* have been translated most frequently, many other works of Augustine show the variations of the translator's art. As we make our rounds of the different aspects of his writing we will mention these different translations. However, one utterly different and new translation must be mentioned now, one that brings a totally popular style to his work done by the English Dominican missionary Edmund Hill. Convinced that Augustine could not have been such a popular preacher if he had used in our time the formal Oxford style of Dr. Pusey, Fr. Hill has ventured to produce an immensely readable and at the same time disconcertingly contemporary translation of the *Sermons* of St. Augustine and his great work on the Trinity with engaging and highly informed introductions. His work is aptly called "A Translation for the 21st Century."[4] The reader familiar with the nineteenth-century versions of Augustine may at first feel that he is on a roller coaster, but I have found that Fr. Hill gives me a new appreciation of my old and beloved spiritual guide. The experience of reading Hill's translation makes me think of what it would have been like if Emerson came back from the dead and started to write like William Safire. For example, compare the following translation from *Sermon* 65a with the style of the three selections above:[5]

The proper weight of everything, which carries it where it ought to go, is its love. I mean, it doesn't carry it where it oughtn't to go, but where it ought. Those who love well will be carried off to what they love, and where will that be, but where the good object is which they love? After all, what other reward does Christ the Lord offer when he urges us to love him, but the fulfillment of what he asked the Father for: *I will that where I am, these also may be with me* (Jn 17:24)? Do you want to be where Christ is? Love Christ, and be whirled away to the place of Christ. Something that pulls or whirls you upward doesn't allow you to hurtle downward.

Don't try and invent any other mechanisms for mounting upward; it's by loving that you strive, by loving that you are snatched up and away, by loving that you arrive.

The Critics of Augustine

Since his own time when he engaged in the great controversies (with Donatists who claimed that the sacraments could not be given by repentant clergy who had previously lapsed during the persecutions, and with the Pelagians who really denied the whole supernatural order), St. Augustine has had armies of critics. During his own life they came at him from all sides and even now they still do. It goes beyond the limit of this book to defend him from his present-day critics or even to list them all. Any serious writer who has left five million words is a handy target. Augustine recognized this himself and criticized some of his own positions later on in life when he published his *Retractions* at the age of 72, four years before his death in 430.

It is worth mentioning that the most persistent contemporary criticism of Augustine centers on his belief that no pleasure should be sought apart from the ultimate goal of life which is the blessed possession and vision of God. This attitude is based on Augustine's conviction that God is the highest blessedness, and, if one carefully understands the words, the ultimate pleasure and fulfillment of the human being. His most famous dictum brings this out succinctly: "You have made us for Yourself, O God, and our hearts are restless till they rest in you" (*Confessions* 1.1). Sister Clark very literally translates this text (*quia fecisti nos ad te*) "You have made us *toward* Yourself" and in so doing brings our attention to one of Augustine's central teachings more clearly. Indeed, Augustine thought very simply that God is our ultimate fulfillment, and every pleasure in this life should be directed in some honest way toward attaining that goal. Furthermore, if our lives are properly ordered and the corrupting influences of original sin are overcome by the grace of Christ, our Mediator, what pleasure we do experience and derive from created things will inevitably lead us to God. Beyond that, the proper ordering of our desires for pleasure will bring harmony and love to human relationships, because discord comes from seeking pleasure apart from our final goal. It is very important to know that for St. Augustine human friendship based on mutual love and respect for the child of God in each one is a necessary component of social life; otherwise that life will return to the riotous and competitive world of paganism. Augustine was convinced that friends led those they loved closer to God or they were no friends at all.[6]

Augustine has been accused of being a puritan and antihuman, opposed to the fulfillment of normal human needs like sexual desire. Only those with the most superficial knowledge of Augustine can make this criticism, or those blinded by their own hedonistic philosophies. Peter Brown in his critical biography of Augustine gives a very well-informed opinion:

> Yet given the harsh moral climate of the age, Augustine was a moderate man. He expected that, ideally, intercourse should take place only to conceive children; but this was no more than austere pagans had demanded. He considered that the extreme views of some Christians, that marriage should be a competition in continence, was not applicable to the average man; and he knew very well that it was positively harmful if used by one partner against the other. Yet, twenty years previously, in the mellow mood that had coincided with the writing of the *Confessions*, Augustine had even gone so far as to suggest, with great sensitivity, that the quality of sexual intercourse itself might be modified and transformed by the permanent friendship of two people in marriage.[7]

What is very important to keep in mind is that in Augustine's time, as in many other times, women were often seen as the servants of men's sexual needs. Augustine as bishop railed against some men in his own congregation who were otherwise decent and respectful to their wives but kept a concubine in the house for their own indulgence. Augustine was unequivocal with the rationalism "surely I can do what I want in my own house." Augustine answered, "No, you cannot. People who do that go straight to Hell."[8]

Brown says that Augustine, who had lived by this double standard before his conversion by having a mistress he could not legally marry and who had repented of it publicly in his *Confessions*, took up the challenge of concubinage in his sermons. He protested that no Christian woman had to put up with this. He said to these unfaithful husbands: "I solemnly warn you, I lay down this rule, I command you. I command you as your bishop; and it is Christ who commands me." He softened his rebuke by observing that as bishop he had heard of all the adulterers but not about all those who were being faithful to Christ.[9]

Because Augustine was one of the founders of religious life in the West and often wrote in support of the vowed life, he is sometimes presented as opposed to marriage by those unaware that he wrote a whole book on Christian marriage. Although like many ecclesiastical and spiritual writers he saw the vowed celibate life as closer to the Gospel counsels and the ideal presented by St. Paul, he readily admitted the superiority of a humble housewife over a proud nun.

The Life of a Writer

Augustine's life is so entwined with his writing that one really cannot be studied without the other. The readers seeking to discover Augustine as a spiritual writer are best served in this volume if we explore his writings and life together. This will most easily be done in chapter 1 when we study the first thirty-five years of Augustine's life, which are the subject of the *Confessions*. In his later years as a writer and bishop it is not so simple to trace his development because Augustine's principal concern is not to give an account of his spiritual journey but to respond to the various needs of the church and the times in which he lived. His two other masterpieces, *The Trinity* and *The City of God*, were both composed in response to needs of the Christian community; but like all other works of creative genius they reflect what the writer was deeply experiencing at the time of composition. It is a difficult and challenging endeavor to try to summarize in a few pages a life as rich as St. Augustine's. The following sketch is meant to provide for those who are not able to read a good biography of the saint at this moment.

A Cameo of Augustine

The fascinating portrait provided by John Lynch as the cover for this book shows a strong man with Italian features, a passionate yet gentle face suffused with light from above. The portrait itself raises questions and poses apparent contradictions especially for the devout who are accustomed to think of saints as rather bland people with refined features glowing with supernatural virtues. The portraits of saints often remind one, sadly, of pasteurized American cheese. A few have escaped this artistic homogenization—St. Paul (passionate), St. Jerome (austere and almost crabby), St. Francis and St. Catherine of Siena (ecstatic), and St. Thomas More (coolly detached). St. Augustine, on the other hand, is customarily shown with fine aristocratic features and in the somber pose of a bishop. He suffered from having a too enthusiastic liturgical tailor. These paintings fail completely to capture the face of the passionate converted public sinner who saw his role as bishop as being a dedicated servant of the people of God. He abhorred clerical affluence and put on no airs of piosity and was, one might say, someone who called a spade a spade. The drama of Augustine's life is that this most unlikely candidate for sanctity was hit with a bolt of divine grace and was gradually transformed by what he called "the light of God."

Augustine described this central experience of his life, the illumination by grace, in the following way: "What is that light which shines upon me but not continuously, and strikes my heart with no wounding? I draw back in terror; I am on fire with longing; terror insofar as I am different from it, longing in the degree of my likeness to it. It is wisdom itself, which in those moments shines upon me, cleaving through my cloud (*Confessions* 11.9)."

If the cover of this volume with its earthy, passionate face suffused by a light from above strikes you as a bit incongruous, know that the man we study illustrates more than many others the apparent incongruity of grace. This face bears the marks of one who experienced the same mystery that caused St. Paul to know that where sin abounded grace did more abound and that power is made perfect in weakness.

The Deceptively Simple Facts

Aurelius Augustinus was born in 354 in Thagaste, an old town in the Roman colonial province of Numidia, not far from the north coast of Africa (now Algeria). His father, Patricius, was a somewhat unsuccessful businessman with upper-middle-class aspirations. His mother, Monica, was a woman of great faith and determination, an utterly dedicated Christian, and in terms of her independence of thought and action, a woman far ahead of her own times. Because of the heroic qualities portrayed by her son in the *Confessions,* Monica is honored as a saint of the Catholic Church and is commemorated on August 27, the day preceding the feast of St. Augustine.

Augustine grew up an official catechumen, that is, someone waiting for the appropriate time to make a formal application for baptism, which, according to custom, was given only to infants when they were in danger of death. In fact, by the time he was of age to make a serious request for baptism, Augustine was becoming a dissolute and brilliant member of the intelligentsia of the declining Roman Empire. He had left behind the faith his mother had tried to give to him and went from a life of immoral worldliness as a young student of rhetoric to a devotee of the Manichees, a rather exotic cult who viewed all material things as obstacles to the soul on its journey to the principle of the dualistic divinity of good and evil. Soon Augustine, now in his twenties, settled down with a concubine to whom he was faithful, and a son, Adeodatus, became disgusted with Manichaeism because it offered no possibility of spiritual development.

As a successful teacher of rhetoric (we would call him today a professor), he taught in North Africa, then in Rome, and finally in

Milan. He embraced the Neoplatonic philosophical religious movement, which, despite its opposition to Christianity, actually led him and a number of his friends closer to accepting Christ and the church. The great drama of his conversion, his separation from the mother of Adeodatus whom he could not marry because of social custom, his failure to achieve a chaste life, his incredible intellectual and emotional conflict, and his sudden conversion are the central theme of the *Confessions*.

Augustine, his son, and his old friend Alypius were baptized by St. Ambrose, archbishop of Milan, at the Easter Vigil on the night of April 25, 387. Although his career as a professor ended with great relief, a totally unforeseen future awaited him. He returned to Africa by way of Rome, where Monica died filled with joy not only at the conversion but also at the obvious spiritual development of her son. Augustine began writings in defense of Christianity, including one called *The Morals of the Catholic Church*, and the first volume of his work on free will. He returned to Africa, going first to Carthage then home to Thagasde, where he and Alypius continued to work on the establishment of a community of Christian men called *Servi Dei*, the "Servants of God." They gathered a little group of men on Augustine's portion of the family estate and attempted to lead a prayerful, contemplative life.

The Catholic Church in this area was surrounded by enemies and critics—pagans, Manichees, and Donatist schismatics. It is not surprising that the church would conscript clergy from this group of well-educated and devout young converts. Augustine was careful to avoid cities where they were looking for a bishop, so he chose the small city of Hippo to set up a monastery of the Servants of God. To quote his own words, "I felt secure because this place already had a bishop. I was grabbed. I was made a priest . . . and then from there I became your bishop."[10]

Beginning as an auxiliary to the aged bishop Valerius, Augustine took on the enemies of the Catholic Church one by one. He was a most effective debater and popular speaker. He even composed a popular song against the teaching of the Donatists. He expounded the Creed to the bishops of Africa and this endeavor became his early book *On True Religion*. He opened his monastery of the Servants of God, and when he succeeded Valerius, he required that all new priests be members of this monastic brotherhood. Other members of the Servants of God became bishops in Africa and, in fact, the whole ecclesiastical picture in that vast area began to change for the better with Augustine as its dominant figure.

Augustine served, and this word is precisely accurate, as bishop of Hippo from 395 to his death in 430. Except to go to church councils, he rarely left the city. He labored tirelessly and wrote prolifically. He was particularly dedicated to the care of the poor. The great literary milestones of his ministry are the publication of the *Confessions* in 401, the final and difficult completion of *The Trinity* in 420, and the publication of *The City of God* in sections from 413 to 425.

Augustine died on August 28, 430, as the Arian vandals were destroying Roman Africa and actually laying siege to Hippo. The details of his death and many events of his life will emerge as our exploration of his writing unfolds. Augustine remains one of the towering intellectual figures of Western civilization and, in fact, of all human history. He is one of the greatest fathers of the church and is often depicted with Leo the Great, Jerome, and Gregory the Great as one of the four preeminent fathers of the church in the West. Throughout his life he considered himself a penitential sinner, saved only by Christ, and a servant of God. As a bishop he sought only to be a good shepherd who willingly and with incredible energy and effort laid down his life for the flock of Christ.

Chapter One

The Young Augustine—
The *Confessions*

A year before his death the aged Augustine made a gift of a copy of the *Confessions* to Count Darius, an imperial agent who had written him a letter expressing his great esteem. The epistle accompanying this gift reveals the whole tenor of the book and of Augustine's own estimate of himself throughout his life, so to speak, his self image. "In these (scrolls) take a look at me that you may not go beyond in your praise what I really am; believe what is said of me here, not by others, but by myself. In this book think about me and see what I have been in myself and by myself . . . because 'He made us and not we ourselves,' in fact, we have brought ourselves to ruin, and He who made us once has made us new all over again."[1] The *Confessions* is the deeply moving account of a brilliant but dissolute man and his encounter with God and His grace.

It is often claimed that next to the Bible itself the *Confessions of St. Augustine* is the most widely read and influential Christian's book ever written. The author is acknowledged by many as the greatest father of the church, or at least of the church in the West.[2] At the heart of his influence is this single work, the first psychological autobiography in human history. No similar writing is to be found in world literature, examining the functions, thoughts, feelings, and even unconscious dynamics of the inner person, until the late Renaissance, twelve hundred years later. If this is your first real attempt at reading the *Confessions* with serious attention (as with the Bible, everyone knows the story), you must read it, as Augustine would say, with the eyes of your heart, that is, with the prayerful and meditative attention that such a work of spiritual genius requires.

The *Confessions* were written around the year 397, about two years after Augustine had become coadjutor (or auxiliary) bishop of Hippo, a Roman colonial city of moderate size in North Africa. A cluster had formed of Roman gentlemen and teachers who had recently become converts or had at least started to take their Christianity seriously. They were called the Servants of God and had begun writing the accounts of their personal acceptance of their faith in Christ. These books were all entitled *Confessions*. Paulinus, who would later become bishop of Nola, among others influenced Augustine to write his confessions, never dreaming that such a revealing, such an emotionally gripping, so brilliant an account of the mind would come forth. Brown states that none of the other Servants of God wrote a book even remotely resembling Augustine's *Confessions*.[3] Perhaps the best assessment of the *Confessions* is given by Augustine himself over thirty years later, shortly before his death. Speaking of the *Confessions* as praise of the just and good God who sought him in his good and evil ways, Augustine writes that they "move the mind and feelings of men through the Lord." Then he reveals that "they had this effect on me when I wrote them and they still do when I read them now."[4]

Two Important Elements

Before picking up the *Confessions* it is helpful that the reader should be prepared to be sensitive to certain important elements in this book.

First, you ought to observe the immense power of the mind with which you are dealing. When I first picked my way through Pusey's translation at fourteen, I had the same feeling I experienced when I read St. Paul—I was being pulled along by a powerful or rather irresistible current. I felt that I was touching reality on the inside—not on the surface of things, however valuable the knowledge of that surface may be.

Reading the *Confessions* and then reading some other great spiritual books is similar to me to the experience of first reading the Gospel of John and then reading the Gospel of Mark. Both of these Gospels are revealed, and each is obviously helpful in its own way. Both are beautiful and captivating. But in the *Confessions*, as in John's Gospel, you put your hand on the Word of God, and you experience creation from inside. An eminent modern disciple of Augustine, Romano Guardini, in his work *The Conversion of Augustine*, which you should read later, calls this mysterious quality of Augustine "inwardness."

> [Augustinian inwardness] is not emotional, labyrinthine, or farfetched. It has clarity of thought, ardor of heart, depth of understanding. The world's vastness is reflected in it, touching it with the cosmic. It knows itself related to the realm of eternal images, which in the Logos are norm and tool of creation. In it too is a consciousness of history, the awareness of leadership and responsibility which lend it personal earnestness.[5]

The second element to which the reader must be sensitive is the interplay, always engaging and sometimes confusing, between intelligence and reason on the one hand and feeling, emotion, and intuition on the other. In a metaphor this is the dialogue between mind and heart. Depending on who you are, certain passages will shine with intelligence or glow with feeling. In the selections I propose in this chapter for your initial experience of the *Confessions,* I will be more inclined to select passages that are intuitive and emotionally powerful. They will also be brilliantly intelligent and filled with the effects of grace, inspired in the secondary sense of that word, that is not inspired like Scripture but by grace. I will avoid suggesting passages in which Augustine explains and demolishes the teaching of the Manichees or other less exotic movements. Later on, when the reader is better prepared, having read at least a biography and some introductory notes to the book, the time will be right "to plow through" and read the whole *Confessions.* Presently our goal is to identify what is best for comfortable spiritual reading.

After choosing one of several good modern translations available you should be able to follow our outline. We will be concentrating on the Augustinian theme of finding and responding to God as He calls to us through the things known by sense and intelligence. God's beauty and splendor leads each of us to

Himself once the way has been prepared by the grace of Christ, the divine and human Mediator. The road we will travel with Augustine in the *Confessions* is historical in the sense that the book covers the first three decades of his life in chronological order. The key quotations will be given in the text, but the reader is advised to fill in the powerful connecting sections by using a translation with the chapters numbered in the usual way.

Book I—Infancy to Adolescence

The *Confessions* is a prayer addressed almost entirely to God. Following Sheed's translation, the opening prayer sets the tone for the whole book. The burden of the meaning of this opening prayer is that we must be led by God himself who has made us toward "himself," otherwise we may be worshiping a false God of our making.

Great art Thou, O Lord, and greatly to be praised; great is Thy power, and of Thy wisdom there is no number. And man desires to praise Thee. He is but a tiny part of all that Thou has created. He bears about him his mortality, the evidence of his sinfulness, and the evidence that Thou dost resist the proud: yet this tiny part of all that Thou has created desires to praise Thee.

Thou dost so excite him that to praise Thee is his joy. For Thou hast made us for Thyself and our hearts are restless till they rest in Thee. (*Confessions* 1.1)

Augustine pauses at the beginning of this great prayer to ask who the real God is—God who has been revealed to human beings as above all things. This prayer is all the more important since it is written in a society that was still half pagan by a man escaping from paganism.

What then is my God, what but the Lord God? For Who is Lord but the Lord, or Who is God but our God? O Thou, the greatest and the best, mightiest, almighty, most merciful and most just, utterly hidden and utterly present, most beautiful and most strong, abiding yet mysterious, suffering no change and changing all things: never new, never old, making all things new, bringing age upon the proud and they know it not; ever in action, ever at rest, gathering all things to Thee and needing none; sustaining and fulfilling and protecting, creating and nourishing and making perfect; ever seeking though lacking nothing. (*Conf.* 1.4)

After describing his infancy and raising some very interesting questions about this time of life, Augustine confronts the semipaganism of his own time. He almost ironically asks questions about cultural assumptions that are as pertinent to our times as they were to his.

O God, my God, what emptiness and mockeries did I now experience: for it was impressed upon me as right and proper in a boy to obey those who taught me, that I might get on in the world and excel in the handling of words to gain honor among men and deceitful riches. I, poor wretch, could not see the use of the things I was sent to school to learn; but if I proved idle in learning, I was soundly beaten.

As a boy I fell into the way of calling upon You, my Help and my Refuge; and in those prayers I broke the strings of my tongue — praying to You, small as I was but with no small energy, that I might not be beaten at school. (*Conf.* 1.9)

Frequently, Augustine will return to the theme of the vanity of his education and to the false values that were imparted to him. This theme may make the reader uneasy. Is it too much, is it too severe? These prayers set the stage for the journey upward to God. Years later Augustine would observe that you will never become what you ought to be unless you are dissatisfied with what you are now.

Yet is was no wonder that I fell away into vanity and went so far from Thee, my God, seeing that men were held up as models for my imitation who were covered with shame if, in relating some act of theirs in no way evil, they fell into some barbarism or grammatical solecism: yet were praised, and delighted to be praised, when they told of their lusts, provided they did so in correct words correctly arranged. All these things Thou seest, O Lord, and are silent: for Thou art patient and plenteous in mercy and truth. But wilt Thou always stay silent? Even now thou dost draw out of this pit of horror the soul that seeks Thee and thirsts for Thy joys, the heart that says to Thee I have sought Thy face: Thy face, Lord, will I still seek: for to be darkened in heart is to be far from Thy face. (*Conf.* 1.18)

As Augustine recalls his childhood and discovers in it the roots of the disordered life he was going to lead, he also recognized the development of personal qualities, love of truth and goodness, that will eventually bring him closer to the loving knowledge of God decades later. God speaks to him through his young life.

Yet, Lord, I should have owed thanks to You, my God and the most excellent Creator and Ruler of the Universe, even if it had been Your will that I should not live beyond boyhood. For even then I was; I lived: I felt: even so early I had an instinct for the care of my own being, a trace in me of that most profound Unity whence my being was derived; in my interior sense I kept guard over the integrity of my outward sense perception, and in my small thoughts upon small matters I had come to delight in the truth. Therefore He who made me is good and He is my God: and in Him I shall exult for all the good qualities that even as a boy I had. But in this lay my sin: that I sought pleasure, nobility, and truth not in God but in the beings He had created, myself and others. Thus I fell into sorrow and confusion and error. Thanks be to Thee, my Joy and my Glory and my Hope and my God: thanks be to Thee for Thy gifts: but do Thou preserve them in me. (*Conf.* 1.20)

Note: See book 1, chapters 9–19.

Book II—Adolescent Confusion

Adolescence brings Augustine to a full-scale pursuit of happiness through the pleasures of the senses and the mind. His strong need and gift for friendship brings him joy and sorrow, especially since friendship becomes clouded with lust and the self-centered use of others.

My one delight was to love and to be loved. But in this I did not keep the measure of mind to mind, which is the luminous line of friendship; but from the muddy concupiscence of the flesh and the hot imagination of puberty mists steamed up to becloud and darken my heart so that I could not distinguish the white light of love from the fog of lust. Both love and lust boiled within me, and swept my youthful immaturity over the precipice of evil desires to leave me half drowned in a whirlpool of abominable sins. Your wrath had grown mightily against me and I knew it not. I had grown deaf from the clanking of the chain of my mortality, the punishment for the pride of my soul: and I departed further from You, and You left me to myself: and I was tossed about and wasted and poured out and boiling over in my fornications: and You were silent, O my late won Joy. (*Conf.* 2.2)

Augustine becomes aware of beauty, material and intellectual, and even the bonds of friendship. Looking back at his life from the perspective of having been an active Christian for ten years and a bishop for two, he can see that both immoderation and a disordered view of good things in their relationship to God caused him to find grief. Yet he never lost his appreciation for beauty, as is witnessed by his later writings.

There is an appeal to the eye in beautiful things, in gold and silver and all such; the sense of touch has its own powerful pleasures; and the other senses find qualities in things suited to them. Worldly success has its glory, and the power to command and to overcome: and from this springs the thirst for revenge. But in our quest of all these things, we must not depart from you, Lord, or deviate from Your Law. This life we live here below has its own attractiveness, grounded in the measure of beauty it has its harmony with the beauty of all lesser things. The bond of human friendship is admirable, holding many souls as one. Yet in the enjoyment of all such things we commit sin if through immoderate inclination to them—for though they are good, they are of the lowest order of good—things higher and better are forgotten, even You, O Lord our God, and Your Truth and Your Law. These lower things have their delights but not such as my God has, for He made them all. (*Conf.* 2.5)

One evening Augustine and his friends stole the pears from the tree of a neighboring farmer. They destroyed the fruit, for the most part untasted in an act of vandalism. This incident bothered

Augustine twenty-five years later because of its wanton evil. Meditating on it he is drawn ever more to the beauty and justice of God.

Who can unravel that complex, twisted knottedness? It is unclean. I hate to think of it or look at it. I long for Thee, O Justice and Innocence, Joy and Beauty of the clear of sight, I long for Thee with unquenchable longing. There is sure repose in Thee and life untroubled. He that enters into Thee, enters into the joy of his Lord and shall not fear and shall be well in Him who is the Best. I went away from Thee, my God, in my youth I strayed too far from Thy sustaining power, and I became to myself a barren land. (*Conf.* 2.10)

Note: See all of book 2.

Book III—A Student Away from Home

Augustine goes to Carthage, "a cauldron of illicit loves." His mother, Monica, grieves for him because along with his wildness he joins the esoteric, semipagan sect of the Manichees. Monica is in great grief and refuses to live with him but changes her mind when in a dream she is shown that her son will share the same rule of faith. Monica would pray fervently for more than a decade with a hope based on this dream.

And you sent Your hand from above, and raised my soul out of that depth of darkness, because my mother, Your faithful one, wept to You for me more bitterly than mothers weep for the bodily deaths of their children. For by the faith and the spirit which she had from You, she saw me as dead; and You heard her, Lord. You heard her and did not despise her tears when they flowed down and watered the earth against which she pressed her face wherever she prayed. You heard her. What else could have been the cause of that dream by which You so comforted her that she consented to live with me and to eat at the same table in the house: which previously she had refused to do, because she shunned and detested the blasphemies of my error. (*Conf.* 3.11)

See chapters 1, 4, 11, and 12 of book 3.

Book IV—Death of a Friend

When Augustine returns to his hometown of Tagaste to teach rhetoric and live with his mistress, he renews an old friendship. The two friends share much together, but suddenly his friend falls ill and is baptized in danger of death. After he recovers Augustine makes fun of his baptism, and the young man "looked at me as if I were a deadly enemy and in a burst of independence that startled me, warned me that if I wished to continue as his friend I must cease that kind of talk." Later, when Augustine is absent, his friend dies. Augustine describes his suffering.

My heart was black with grief. Whatever I looked upon had the air of death. My native place was a prison-house and my home a strange unhappiness. The things we had done together became sheer torment without him. My eyes were restless looking for him, but he was not there. I hated all places because he was not in them. They could not say "He will come soon," as they would in his life when he was absent. I became a great enigma to myself and I was forever asking my soul why it was sad and why it disquieted me so sorely. And my soul knew not what to answer me. If I said "Trust in God" my soul did not obey—naturally, because the man whom she had loved and lost was nobler and more real than the imagined deity in whom I was bidding her trust. I had no delight but in tears, for tears had taken the place my friend had held in the love of my heart. (*Conf.* 4.4)

From this experience, Augustine begins to learn that he must not place his ultimate happiness in any human being—but in God who does not change. It is a paradox in Augustine's life that he loves only in God, but he loves much more in God than most people even love without putting God first.

This is the root of our grief when a friend dies, and the blackness of our sorrow, and the steeping of the heart in tears for the joy that has turned to bitterness, and the feeling as though we were dead because he is dead. Blessed is the man that loves Thee, O God, and his friend in Thee, and his enemy for Thee. For he alone loses no one that is dear to him, if all are dear in God who is never lost. And who is that God but our God, the God who made heaven and earth, who fills them because it is by filling them with Himself that he has made them? No man loses Thee, unless he goes from Thee; and in going from Thee, where does he go or where does he flee save from Thee to Thee. . . . Wherever the soul of man turns, unless towards God, it cleaves to sorrow, even though the things outside God and outside itself to which it cleaves may be things of beauty. For these lovely things would be nothing at all unless they were from Him. They rise and set; in their rising they begin to be, and they grow towards perfection, and once come to perfection they grow old, and they die: not all grow old but all die. . . . In all such things let my soul praise You, O God, Creator of all things, but let it not cleave too close in love to them through the senses of the body. For they go their way and are no more; and they rend the soul with desires that can destroy it, for it longs to be one with the things it loves and to repose in them. But in them is no place of repose, because they do not abide. They pass, and who can follow them with any bodily sense? Or who can grasp them firm even while they are still here? (*Conf.* 4.9, 10)

Augustine by suffering is beginning to learn that our desires must ever be directed higher—to love all things in God is the only way to keep them, but God's love must be first.

Augustine brings into his account his faith, a faith that he did not have when his friend died. This affirmation of faith illustrates very well the basic Augustinian teaching that we can only find our way to life and eternal happiness through Christ, our divine Mediator.

But our Life came down to this our earth and took away our death, slew death with the abundance of His own life: and He thundered, calling to us to return to Him into that secret place from which He came forth to us—coming first into the Virgin's womb, where humanity was wedded to Him, our mortal flesh, though not always to be mortal; and thence like a bridegroom coming out of his bride chamber, rejoicing as a giant to run his course. For He did not delay but rushed on, calling to us by what He said and what He did, calling to us by His death, life, descent, and ascension to return to Him. And he withdrew from our eyes, that we might return to our own heart and find Him. For He went away and behold He is still here. He would not be with us long, yet He did not leave us. He went back to that place which He had never left, for the world was made by Him. And He was in this world, and He came into this world to save sinners. Unto Him my soul confesses and He hears it, for it has sinned against Him. O ye sons of men, how long will ye be so slow of heart? Even now when Life has come down to you, will you not ascend and live? (*Conf.* 4.12)

Note: See book 4, chapters 1–12.

Book V—From Carthage to Rome and Milan

In this book, which covers his twenty-eighth year, Augustine tells of his escape from the Manichees and his old dissolute companions by going to Rome, where he almost died of an illness. Finally, he becomes a professor in Milan and meets the great bishop St. Ambrose. He is drawn closer to the faith in Christ and signs up as a catechumen, although still living an immoral life. Writing later Augustine puts his doctrine of our ascent to God into this following prayer:

Receive the sacrifice of my Confessions offered by my tongue, which Thou didst form and hast moved to confess unto Thy name. Heal Thou all my bones and they shall say: Lord, who is like to Thee? A man who makes confession to Thee does not thereby give Thee any information as to what is happening within him. The closed heart does not close out Thy eye, nor the heart's hardness resist Thy hand. For Thou dost open it at Thy pleasure whether for mercy or for justice, and there is nothing that can hide itself from Thy heat. But let my soul praise Thee that it may love Thee, and let it tell Thee Thy mercies that it may praise Thee. Without ceasing Thy whole creation speaks Thy praise—the spirit of every man by the words that his mouth directs to Thee, animals and lifeless matter by the mouth of those who look upon them: that so our soul rises out of its mortal weariness unto Thee, helped upward by the things Thou hast made and passing beyond them unto Thee who hast wonderfully made them: and there refreshment is and strength unfailing. (*Conf.* 5.1)

Note: See book 5, chapters 1, 2, 8, 9, 13, 14.

Book VI—Augustine in Milan

Augustine comes to Milan with his mother and his mistress. His mind is still searching for God. He listens to Ambrose and begins to appreciate both the Catholic faith and the vanity of worldly reputation. He is forced to send his mistress of fifteen years back to Africa, but he cannot remain chaste until his planned marriage. He is completely miserable and prays to God.

Meanwhile my sins were multiplied. She with whom I had lived so long was torn from my side as a hindrance to my forthcoming marriage. My heart which had held her very dear was broken and wounded and shed blood. She went back to Africa, swearing that she would never know another man, and left with me the natural son I had had of her. But I in my unhappiness could not, for all my manhood, imitate her resolve. I was unable to bear the delay of two years which must pass before I was to get the girl I had asked for in marriage. In fact it was not really marriage that I wanted. I was simply a slave to lust.

Praise be to Thee, glory to Thee, O fountain of mercies. I became more wretched and Thou more close to me. Thy right hand was ready to pluck me from the mire and wash me clean, though I knew it not. So far nothing called me back from the depth of the gulf of carnal pleasure save fear of death and of the judgment to come, which, through all the fluctuations of my opinions, never left my mind . . . my soul turned and turned again, on back and sides and belly, and the bed was always hard. For Thou alone are her rest. And behold Thou are close at hand to deliver us from the wretchedness of error and establish us in Thy way, and console us with Thy word: "Run, I shall bear you up and bring you and carry you to the end." (*Conf.* 6.15,16)

Note: See book 6, chapters 1, 2, 4, 6, 11–16.

Book VII—Prelude to Conversion

In this book Augustine describes a number of weighty issues that come to his mind as he prepares for conversion. Such problems as

the origin and nature of evil, free will and the nature of God pre-
occupy him. He also realizes the absolute need for Christ. He is
moved by the humility of Christ and his promise to lead us on the
way. He is especially helped by the "latest apostle, Paul."

So I set about finding a way to gain the strength that was necessary for enjoying You. And I could not find it until I embraced the
Mediator between God and man, the man Christ Jesus, who is
over all things, God blessed forever, who was calling unto me and
saying: I am the Way, the Truth, and the Life; and who brought
into union with our nature that Food which I lacked the strength to
take: for the Word was made flesh that Your Wisdom, by which
You created all things, might give suck to our souls' infancy. For I
was not yet lowly enough to hold the lowly Jesus as my God, nor
did I know what lesson his embracing of our weakness was to
teach. For Your Word, the eternal Truth, towering above the highest parts of Your creation, lifts up to Himself those that were cast
down. He built for Himself here below a lowly house of our clay,
that by it He might bring down from themselves and bring up to
Himself those who were to be made subject, healing the swollen-
ness of their pride and fostering their love: so that their self-confi-
dence might grow no further but rather diminish, seeing the deity
at their feet, humbled by the assumption of our coat of human
nature: to the end that weary at last they might cast themselves
down upon His humanity and rise again in its rising. (*Conf.* 7.18)

As Augustine approaches the obedience of faith he begins to
see that the Platonist philosophers, although they sought and recognized many philosophical truths, could not lead him to peace
any more than the Manichees. Only Christ could bring him to salvation.

It is one thing to see the land of peace from a wooded mountain-
top, yet not find the way to it and struggle hopelessly far from the
way, with hosts of those fugitive deserters from God, under their
leader the Lion and the Dragon, besetting us about and ever lying
in wait; and quite another to hold to the way that leads there, a
way guarded by the care of our heavenly General, where there
are no deserters from the army of heaven to practice their rob-
beries—for indeed they avoid that way as a torment. Marvelously

these truths graved themselves in my heart when I read that latest of Your apostles and looked upon Your works and trembled. (*Conf.* 7.21)

Note: In book 7 it will be helpful to read chapters 18–21. We will return later to the very important passages in chapter 10 that deeply affect Augustine's teachings on spirituality.

Book VIII—Conversion

This book contains the most powerful account of a Christian conversion since the New Testament description of the conversion of St. Paul. Augustine's intellectual difficulties gradually become resolved, but he cannot conquer his lust. Finally "in an instant" he is prepared to accept what St. Paul teaches in Romans 13:13, "to make no provision for the flesh and its lusts." His mother rejoices with "triumphant exultation."

The following chapters, which are quoted here extensively, contain a masterpiece of psychological description as well as a profound spiritual statement.

Thus I was sick at heart and in torment, accusing myself with a new intensity of bitterness, twisting and turning in my chain in the hope that it might be utterly broken, for what held me as so small a thing! But it still held me. And You stood in the secret places of my soul, O Lord, in the harshness of Your mercy redoubling the scourges of fear and shame lest I should give way again and that small slight tie which remained should not be broken but should grow again to full strength and bind me closer even than before. For I kept saying within myself: "Let it be now, let it be now," and by the mere words I had begun to move towards the resolution. I almost made it, yet I did not quite make it. But I did not fall back into my original state, but as it were stood near to get my breath. I still shrank from dying unto death and living unto life.

Those trifles of all trifles, and vanities of vanities, my one-time mistress, held me back, plucking at my garment of flesh and murmuring softly: "Are you sending us away?" And "From this moment shall we not be with you, now or forever? And "From this moment shall this or that not be allowed you, now or forever?" What were they suggesting to me in the phrase I have written "this or that," what were they suggesting to me, O my God? Do you in Your mercy keep from the soul of Your servant the vileness and uncleanness they were suggesting. And now I began to hear them not half so loud; they no longer stood against me face to face, but were softly muttering behind my back and, as I tried to depart, plucking stealthily at me to make me look behind. Yet even that was enough, so hesitating was I, to keep me from snatching myself free, from shaking them off and leaping upwards on the way I was called: for the strong force of habit said to me: "Do you think you can live without them?"

When my most searching scrutiny had drawn up all my vileness from the secret depths of my soul and heaped it in my heart's sight, a mighty storm arose in me, bringing a mighty rain of tears. That I might give way to my tears and lamentations, I rose from Alypius: for it struck me that solitude was more suited to the business of weeping. . . . And much I said not in these words but to this effect: "And Thou, O Lord, how long? How long, Lord; wilt Thou be angry forever? Remember not our former iniquities." For I felt that I was still bound by them. And I continued my miserable complaining: "How long, how long shall I go on saying tomorrow and again tomorrow? Why not now, why not have an end to my uncleanness this very hour?"

Such things I said, weeping in the most bitter sorrow of my heart. And suddenly I heard a voice from some nearby house, a boy's voice or a girl's voice, I do not know: but it was a sort of sing-song repeated again and again, "Take and read, take and read." I ceased weeping and immediately began to search my mind most carefully as to whether children were accustomed to chant these words in any kind of game, and I could not remember that I had ever heard any such thing. Damming back the flood of my tears I arose, interpreting the incident as quite certainly a divine command to open my book of Scripture and read the passage at which I should open. So I was moved to return to the place where Alypius was sitting for I had put down the Apostle's book there when I arose. I snatched it up, opened it and in silence read the passage upon which my eyes first fell: *Not in rioting and drunken-*

*ness, not in chambering and impurities, not in contention and
envy, but put ye on the Lord Jesus Christ and make not provision
for the flesh in its concupiscences.* (Romans xiii, 13) I had no wish
to read further, and no need. For in that instant, with the very ending of the sentence, it was as though a light of utter confidence
shone in all my heart, and all the darkness of uncertainty van-
ished away. Then leaving my finger in the place or marking it by
some other sign, I closed the book and in complete calm told the
whole thing to Alypius and he similarly told me what had been
going on in himself, of which I knew nothing. He asked to see
what I had read. I showed him, and he looked further than I had
read. I had not known what followed. And this is what followed:
"Now him that is weak in faith, take unto you." He applied this to
himself and told me so. And he was confirmed by this message,
and with no troubled wavering gave himself to God's goodwill and
purpose—a purpose indeed most suited to his character, for in
these matters he had been immeasurable better than I.

Then we went in to my mother and told her, to her great joy. We
related how it had come about: she was filled with triumphant
exultation, and praised You who are mighty beyond what we ask
or conceive: for she saw that You had given her more than with all
her pitiful weeping she had ever asked. For You converted me to
Yourself so that I no longer sought a wife nor any of this world's
promises, but stood upon that same rule of faith in which You had
shown me to her so many years before. Thus You changed her
mourning into joy, a joy far richer than she had thought to wish, a
joy much dearer and purer than she had thought to find in grand-
children of my flesh. (*Conf.* 8.11, 12)

Note: See book 8, chapters 1–4.

Book IX—The New Convert and the Death of Monica

Augustine describes rather soberly the steps of his baptism by St.
Ambrose. His son Adeodatus and Alypius are baptized with him,
and all anxiety of the past flees away. Monica and Augustine
share a deeply contemplative experience at Ostia as they prepare
to return to Africa. Augustine uses this experience to illustrate

the individual's ascent to God, the focus of our present selection. His central teaching, namely, that we will rise from the beauty of the senses and the splendor of the mind to the contemplation of God, is powerfully illustrated by this experience.

The following passage, called the "Episode at the Window in Ostia," is one of the most celebrated descriptions of the contemplative mystical experience in world literature.

When the day was approaching on which she was to depart this life—a day that You knew though we did not—it came about, as I believe by Your secret arrangement, that she and I stood alone leaning in a window, which looked inward to the garden within the house where we were staying, at Ostia on the Tiber; for there we were away from everybody, resting for the sea-voyage from the weariness of our long journey by land. There we talked together, she and I alone, in deep joy; and *forgetting the things that were behind and looking forward to those that were before,* we were discussing in the presence of Truth, which You are, what the eternal life of the saints could be like, which eye has not seen nor ear heard, nor has it entered into the heart of man. But with the mouth of our heart we panted for the high waters of Your fountain, the fountain of the life which is with You: that being sprinkled from that fountain according to our capacity, we might in some sense meditate upon so great a matter.

And our conversation had brought us to this point, that any pleasure whatsoever of the bodily senses, in any brightness whatsoever of corporeal light, seemed to us not worthy of comparison with the pleasure of that eternal Light, not worthy even of mention. Rising as our love flamed upward towards that Selfsame, we passed in review the various levels of bodily things, up to the heavens themselves, whence sun and moon and stars shine upon this earth. And higher still we soared, thinking in our minds and speaking and marvelling at Your works; and so we came to our own souls and went beyond them to come at last to that region of richness unending, where You feed Israel forever with the food of truth: and there life is that Wisdom by which all things are made, both the things that have been and the things that are yet to be. But this Wisdom itself is not made: it is as it has ever been, and so it shall be forever: indeed "has ever been" and "shall be forever" have no place in it, but it simply is, for it is eternal: whereas "to have been" and "to be going to be" are not eternal. And while we were thus talking of His Wisdom and panting for it, with all the effort of our heart we did for one instant attain to touch it; then sighing, and leaving the first fruits of our spirit bound to it, we returned to the sound of our own tongue, in which a word has both beginning and ending. For what is like to Your Word, Our Lord, who abides in Himself for ever, yet grows not old and makes all things new!

So we said: If to any man the tumult of the flesh grew silent, silent the images of earth and sea and air: and if the heavens grew silent, and the very soul grew silent to herself and by not thinking of self mounted beyond self: if all dreams and imagined visions grew silent, and every tongue and every sign and whatsoever is transient—for indeed if any man could hear them, he should hear them saying with one voice: We did not make ourselves but he made us who abides forever: but if, having uttered this and so set us to listening to Him who made them, they all grew silent, and in their silence He alone spoke to us, not by them but by Himself: so that we should hear His word, not by any tongue of flesh nor the voice of an angel nor the sound of thunder nor in the darkness of a parable, but that we should hear Himself whom in all these things we love, should hear Himself and not them: just as we two had but now reached forth and in a flash of the mind attained to touch the eternal Wisdom which abides over all: and if this could continue, and all other visions so different be quite taken away, and this one should so ravish and absorb and wrap the beholder in inward joys that his life should eternally be such as that one moment of understanding for which we had been sighing—would not this be: *Enter Thou into the joy of Thy Lord?* But when shall it be? Shall it be when we shall all rise again and shall not all be changed? (*Conf.* 9.10)

Not long after this exquisite experience of mother and son, Monica dies surrounded by her family and at great peace that her son has found God. Augustine is overwhelmed with grief but is also filled with hope. The following passage gives not only his loving thoughts of his mother but a picture of the attitude of a devout early Christian toward those who had died in Christ. This

quotation to this day influences millions of believers in their attitudes toward prayer for their beloved dead.

Now that my heart is healed of that wound, in which there was
perhaps too much of earthly affection, I pour forth to You, O our
God, tears of a very different sort for Your handmaid—tears that
flow from a spirit shaken by the thought of the perils there are for
every soul that dies in Adam. For though she had been made
alive in Christ, and while still in the body had so lived that Your
name was glorified in her faith and her character, yet I dare not
say that from the moment of her regeneration in baptism no word
issued from her mouth contrary to Your Command. Your Son,
who is truth, has said: *Whosoever shall say to his brother, Thou
fool, shall be in danger of hell fire;* and it would go ill with the most
praiseworthy life lived by men, if You were to examine it with Your
mercy laid aside! But because You do not enquire too fiercely into
our sins, we have hope and confidence of a place with You. Yet if
a man reckons up before You the merits he truly has, what is he
reckoning except Your own gifts? If only men would know themselves to be but men, so that he that glories would glory in the
Lord!

Thus, my Glory and my Life, God of my heart, leaving aside for
this time her good deeds, for which I give thanks to Thee in joy, I
now pray to Thee for my mother's sins. Grant my prayer through
the true Medicine of our wounds, who hung upon the cross and
who now sitting at Thy right hand makes intercession for us. I
know that she dealt mercifully, and from her heart forgave those
who trespassed against her: do Thou also forgive such trespasses as she may have been guilty of in all the years since her
baptism, forgive them, Lord, forgive them, I beseech Thee: enter
not into judgment with her. Let Thy mercy be exalted above Thy
justice for Thy words are true and Thou hast promised that the
merciful shall obtain mercy. That they should be merciful is Thy
gift *who hast mercy on whom Thou wilt, and wilt have compassion on whom thou wilt.*

And I believe that Thou hast already done what I am now asking;
but be not offended, Lord, at the things my mouth would utter. For
on that day when her death was so close, she was not concerned

that her body should be sumptuously wrapped or embalmed with spices, nor with any thought of choosing a monument or even for burial in her own country. Of such things she gave us no command, but only desired to be remembered at Thy altar, which she had served without ever missing so much as a day, on which she knew that the holy Victim was offered, *by whom the handwriting is blotted out of the decree that was contrary to us,* by which offering too the enemy was overcome who, reckoning our sins and seeking what may be laid to our charge, found nothing in Him, in whom we are conquerors.

So let her rest in peace, together with her husband, for she had no other before nor after him, but served him, in patience bringing forth fruit for Thee, and winning him likewise for Thee. And inspire, O my Lord my God, inspire Thy servants my brethren, . . . that as many of them as read this may remember at Thy altar Thy servant Monica, with Patricius, her husband, by whose bodies Thou didst bring me into this life, though how I know not. (*Conf.* 9.13)

Note: See all of book 9.

Book X—Augustine Finds God

Augustine's autobiography ends with book 10. The remaining three books of the *Confessions* pertain to philosophical and spiritual topics that we will consider later on. In this tenth book all the strands of Augustine's quest for beauty and truth through the senses, mind, and faith come together. The *Confessions* began with a prayer that he would pray to God who would be known by faith so that he would not "invoke another than Thee, knowing Thee not" (1,1). It is important to recognize that this prayer is written by a man who did not know God for many years and was involved with the false ideas of the Manichees. In book 10 Augustine shows that through the senses, intellect, and the assent of faith in Christ he has been enabled to pray to the true God. This book begins with this prayer, "Let me know Thee who knowest me, let me know Thee as I am known."

Augustine begins his great statement of faith with the realization that God has given him faith and even love. "You have stricken my heart with Your word and I love You." But then he asks what is it that he loves—what is it that has called to him. In the following prayer he poetically questions the things that speak to his senses.

It is with no doubtful knowledge, Lord, but with utter certainty that I love You. You have stricken my heart with Your word and I have loved You. And indeed heaven and earth and all that is in them tell me wherever I look that I should love You, and they cease not to tell it to all men, so that there is no excuse for them. For You will have mercy on whom You will have mercy, and You will show mercy to whom You will show mercy: otherwise heaven and earth cry their praise of You to deaf ears.

But what is it that I love when I love You? Not the beauty of any bodily thing, nor the order of seasons, not the brightness of light that rejoices the eye, nor the sweet melodies of all songs, nor the sweet fragrance of flowers and ointments and spices: not manna nor honey, not the limbs that carnal love embraces. None of these things do I love in loving my God. Yet in a sense I do love light and melody and fragrance and food and embrace when I love my God—the light and the voice and the fragrance and the food and embrace in the soul, when the light shines upon my soul which no place can contain, that voice sounds which no time can take from me, I breathe that fragrance which no wind scatters, I eat the food which is not lessened by eating, and I lie in the embrace which satiety never comes to sunder. This it is that I love, when I love my God.

And, what is this God? I asked the earth and it answered: "I am not He"; and all things that are in the earth made the same confession. I asked the sea and the deeps and the creeping things, and they answered: "We are not your God; seek higher." I asked the winds that blow, and the whole air with all that is in it answered: "Anaximenes (a philosopher) was wrong; I am not God," I asked the heavens, the sun, the moon, the stars, and they answered: "Neither are we God whom you seek." And I said to all the things that throng about the gateways of the senses: "Tell me of my God, since you are not He. Tell me something of Him." And they cried out in a great voice: "He made us." (*Conf.* 10.6)

Augustine in his search for God now goes beyond the senses into the powers of the mind and soul, and he comes to memory, which for him is the location of reason and intelligence. His description of memory needs to be studied by itself, but here we can only allude to it. Again in 10, 7 Augustine asks what it is that he loves when he loves God. "Who is He that is above the topmost point of my soul?" He comes to his rich description of memory.

I shall mount beyond this power of my nature, still rising by degrees towards Him who made me. And so come to the fields and vast palaces of memory, where are stored the innumerable images of material things brought to it by the senses. Further there is stored in the memory the thoughts we think, by adding to or taking from or otherwise modifying the things that sense has made contact with, and all other things that have been entrusted to and laid up in memory, save such as forgetfulness has swallowed in its grave. (*Conf.* 10.8)

After describing many of the functions of the mind he continues:

All this I do inside me, in the huge court of my memory. In my memory are sky and earth and sea, ready at hand along with all the things that I have ever been able to perceive in them and have not forgotten. And in my memory too I meet myself—I recall myself, what I have done, when and where and in what state of mind I was when I did it. In my memory are all the things I remember to have experienced myself or to have been told by others. From the same store I can weave into the past endless new likenesses of things experienced; and from these again I can picture actions and events and hopes for the future; and upon them all I can meditate as if they were present. (*Conf.* 10.8)

Augustine discovers that with all of its mysterious ability memory itself is not where one finds God.

Great is the power of memory, a thing, O my God, to be in awe of, a profound and immeasurable multiplicity; and this thing is my mind, this thing am I. What then am I, O my God? What nature am I? A life powerfully various and manifold and immeasurable. In the innumerable fields and dens and caverns of my memory, innumerably full of innumerable kinds of things, present either by their images as are all bodies, or in themselves as are our mental capacities, or by certain notions or awarenesses, like the affections of the mind.

What am I to do now, O my true Life, my God? I shall mount beyond this my power of memory, I shall mount beyond it, to come to You, O lovely light. What have You to say to me? In my ascent by the mind to You who abide above me, I shall mount up beyond that power of mine called memory, longing to attain to touch You at the point where that contact is possible and to cleave to You at the point where it is possible to cleave. I shall pass beyond memory to find You, O truly good and certain Loveliness, and where shall I find You? If I find You beyond my memory, then shall I be without memory of You. And how shall I find You if I am without memory of You? (*Conf.* 10.17)

Now it comes to Augustine that he does not find God in any place sensible or intellectual, neither in the world or in his mind. We do not find God; rather God finds us. He comes to us and not we to him. The whole journey toward God has been in fact His merciful journey toward us.

In what place then did I find You to learn of You? For You were not in my memory, before I learned of You. Where then did I find You to learn of You save in Yourself, above myself? Place there is none, we go this way and that, and place there is none. You, who are Truth, reside everywhere to answer all who ask counsel of You, and in one act reply to all though all seek counsel upon different matters. And You answer clearly but all do not hear clearly. All ask what they wish, but do not always hear the answer that they wish. That man is Your best servant who is not so much concerned to hear from You what he wills as to will what he hears from You. (*Conf.* 10.26)

With all that we have learned in these ten books we return to the quotation we first considered. How much more meaning it has now, and how it brings together all the strands of Augustine's quest. He has journeyed to God only to discover that God has been constantly with him and seeking for him. The drama does not end here, however. In fact, it begins anew. Having discovered God, or rather having been discovered by him, Augustine tires of life and its struggle and longs simply to be completely united with God. But this is not to be now. He must struggle on with a life drawn to God and directed by God, yet because of his human weakness there is no hope in his doing this except by God's grace. The stage is set for the spiritual combat of the Christian life.

Late have I loved Thee, O beauty so ancient and so new; late have I loved Thee! For behold Thou were within me, and I outside; and I sought Thee outside and in my unloveliness fell upon those lovely things that Thou hast made. Thou were with me and I was not with Thee. I was kept from Thee by those things, yet had they not been in Thee, they would not have been at all. Thou didst call and cry to me and break open my deafness: and Thou didst send forth Thy beams and shine upon me and chase away my blindness: Thou didst breathe fragrance upon me, and I drew in my breath and do now pant for Thee: I tasted Thee, and now hunger and thirst for Thee: Thou didst touch me, and I have burned for Thy peace. (*Conf.* 10.27)

The following prayer may be said to encapsulate the rest of the life of St. Augustine, his years of struggle, labors, and suffering as a bishop. Never did he lose sight of the fact that he had been lost and found again by God. Never did he rely on his own strength of virtue. Never did he run away from what God commands and gives us the strength to do.

All my hope is naught save in thy great mercy. Grant what Thou dost command, and command what Thou wilt. Thou dost command continence. And when I knew, as it is said, that no one could be continent unless God gave it, even this was a point of wisdom, to know whose gift it was. For by continence we are collected and bound up into unity within ourself, whereas we had been scattered abroad in multiplicity. Too little does any man love Thee, who loves some other thing together with Thee, loving it not on account of Thee, O Thou Love, who are ever burning and never extinguished! O Charity, my God, enkindle me! Thou dost command continence: grant what Thou dost command and command what Thou wilt. (*Conf.* 10.29)

Like so many Christians of that troubled time Augustine thought of escaping from the decaying corpse of the Roman Empire and from the wild attacks of the barbarians into solitude. But his love for Christ intervened. He recognized more than most believers of his time that Christ had saved us by his humility and suffering. He was passionately devoted to Christ, and so he stayed in the world as a minister of the gospel and sacraments, as priest and bishop, to befriend all who seek for Christ.

His innate love for friendship became the chain of charity, the *vinculum caritatis,* binding him to help and encourage all of those who had listened to the call of the merciful Savior. This powerful Christian prayer ends the autobiography of St. Augustine and shapes the rest of his years as a servant of Christ and his flock.

But the true Mediator, whom in the secret of Your mercy You have shown to men and sent to men, that by His example they might learn humility—the Mediator between God and men, the man Christ Jesus, appeared between sinful mortals and the immortal Just One: for like men He was mortal, like God He was Just; so that, the wages of justice being life and peace, He might, through the union of His own justice with God, make void the death of those sinners whom He justified by choosing to undergo death as they do. He was shown forth to holy men of old that they might be saved by justice with God, make void the death of those sinners whom He justified by choosing to undergo death as they do. He was shown forth to holy men of old that they might be saved by faith in His Passion to come, now that He has suffered it. As man, He is Mediator; but as Word, He is not something in between, for He is equal to God, God with God, and together one God.

How much Thou has loved us, O good Father, *Who hast spared not even Thine own Son, but delivered Him up for us wicked men!* How Thou has loved us, for whom He who *thought it not robbery to be equal with Thee became obedient even unto the death of the Cross,* He who alone was *free among the dead, having power to lay down His life and power to take it up again;* for us He was to Thee both Victor and Victim, and Victor became Victim: for us He was to Thee both Priest and Sacrifice, and Priest because Sacrifice: turning us from slaves into Thy sons, by being Thy Son and becoming a slave. Rightly is my hope strong in Him, who sits at Thy right hand and intercedes for us; otherwise I should despair. For many and great are my infirmities, many and great; but Thy medicine is of more power. We might well have thought Thy Word remote from union with man and so have despaired of ourselves, if it had not been *made flesh and dwelt among us.*

Terrified by my sins and the mass of my misery, I had pondered in my heart and thought of flight to the desert; but Thou didst forbid me and strengthen me, saying: *And Christ died for all: that they also who live, may now not live to themselves but with Him who died for them.* See, Lord, I cast my care upon Thee, that I may live: *and I will consider the wondrous things of Thy law.* Thou knowest my unskillfulness and my infirmity: teach me and heal me. He thy only One, in whom are hidden all the treasures of wisdom and knowledge, has redeemed me with His blood. *Let not the proud speak evil of me,* for I think upon the price of my redemption, I eat it and drink it and give it to others to eat and drink; and being poor I desire to be filled with it among those that eat and are filled: and they shall praise the Lord that seek Him (*Conf.* 10.43)

Note: See book 10, chapters 1–3, 6–29, 42, and 43.

+ Chapter Two +

Augustine the Philosopher

Those of us who enjoy exploring libraries for great spiritual writings are seldom drawn to the section marked "Philosophy." And those who venture into these remote sections are usually happy to leave for the next stack of books after they have read for a while from a dusty tome. This is unfortunate because most of the great ideas of humanity except those coming directly from revelation are found in philosophy. The average reader may agree that this is all very true but continue to search for his or her personal reading in less demanding volumes.

If you are going to really get something out of the explorations of the Augustinian Alps you should have some appreciation of the saint's philosophy—and if you persevere to the end of this chapter you should emerge from it with a few new ways of thinking about things—and that is what philosophy is supposed to provide. (If you find that his philosophy is beyond your interest at this time, you can go on to the next chapter and perhaps return to this one at the end of this book.)

To return to our earlier analogy of exploring the Augustinian Alps, suppose you were traveling on a moonlit night with snow covered mountain peaks all around you. You could not see the details as clearly as in the day. You would not be able to see the height and mass of the looming peaks as well as in daylight—but you would be enveloped in the mysterious shadows of the panorama. The very fact that much is not seen but is known to be there adds to the silent grandeur of the spectacle. For most of us who have little expertise in philosophy, this sense of intelligent awe in the face of what we do not entirely comprehend is enriching. In the face of ideas whose importance we appreciate while their full implications trail off into shadows like the outline of mountain peaks at night, we may taste what Jacques Maritain called "the metaphysical experience" of philosophy.

Reason, Knowledge, and Wisdom

Many of our readers will have a knowledge of philosophy growing out of the monumental work of St. Thomas Aquinas who rediscovered Aristotle and brought his system of thought into Christianity. This remarkable feat actually laid the foundations for modern science and until recently was what most Catholic college students studied. Augustine, whom Thomas acknowledged as his teacher, had been deeply influenced in his thinking by Plato. Augustine's ideas on human nature, reality, and God were drawn from Scripture, but he fitted them into the Platonic framework—especially his ideas about the nature of human experience, the meaning of history, and the everlasting significance of the individual. In doing this Augustine followed the path of several of the Greek fathers of the church who preceded him, and he set a course that would guide Catholic theology for the next eight hundred years. He could easily justify his use of Platonic ideas to help comprehend the revealed truths of Scripture because these very ideas are to be found in the Gospel of John and in the thought of St. Paul. In order to taste a bit of the spiritual legacy of Augustine's philosophical writings we need to explore a few of his ideas.

As far as human thinking is concerned, Augustine defined some key concepts differently from Aristotle. Reason (*ratio*) is not logical thinking but a gazing by the mind (*aspectus mentis*) leading to a clear impression of the object that is called knowledge.[1] St. Augustine was very clear about two things. The first is that much of what we know we learn and accept from "authority"—the information provided by experts and witnesses and finally by the authority of God himself. We can only function as intelligent human beings because of what we have learned from others. Modern people who have a bias against authority, perhaps because it is so often abused, will find Augustine's emphasis on the "authority" of teachers almost an exotic idea although it is obvious that we constantly learn because of some credence that we give to informants, teachers, and experts. A holy hour at the evening TV watching the news, informative programs, and commercials will reveal in a frightening way just how much authority we unconsciously give to those who form public opinion or to the creators of what is deemed to be correct or stylish. Yet, if we did not learn from others, without having our own direct experience of these things, we would all have to reinvent the wheel. The second of Augustine's key thoughts is that knowledge leads to understanding—whether we get the knowledge from authority or from our experience. Understanding, including appreciation, is very important in his thought.

Augustine lived at a time when philosophy, Scripture, and religious belief were not considered distinct. Most thinkers pursued wisdom, a knowledge of life that would lead to blessedness and even to a permanent state of beatitude beyond this life. The following quotation from Augustine's work *Against the Academics* illustrates his psychological quest pursuing the comprehensive path to wisdom using reason and faith together but always putting revelation in the lead. This procedure may strike a Thomist or a nonbeliever pursuing the knowledge of truth as a confusion of the two sources of rational examination and belief. That objection would not have occurred to Augustine and his contemporaries, who saw the pursuit of wisdom in a more holistic way. Christians and non-Christians accepted that you could use all of your valid experience (not folly or delusion) in the struggle for wisdom.

And now—that you may grasp my whole meaning in a few words—whatever may be the nature of human wisdom, I see that I have not yet understood it. Nevertheless, although I am now in the thirty-third year of my life, I do not think that I ought to despair of understanding it some day, for I have resolved to disregard all the other things which mortals consider good, and to devote myself to an investigation of it. Certainly, no one doubts that we are impelled toward knowledge by a two-fold force; the force of authority and the force of reason. And I am resolved never to deviate in the least from the authority of Christ, for I find none more powerful. But, as to what is attainable by acute and accurate reasoning, such is my state of mind that I am impatient to grasp what truth is—to grasp it not only by belief, but also by comprehension. (*Against the Academics* 3.20.43)

This quotation focuses our attention on a central theme of Augustine that would affect all Christian theology: that is, faith seeking understanding. Augustine's pursuit of wisdom contrasts sharply with how philosophy is defined in contemporary academia—even Christian intellectual circles. Augustine's approach, indeed that of the fathers, might be ridiculed as a form of fundamentalism except for the fact that Augustine required the full use of reason in the exploration of revealed knowledge. Augustine is neither a rationalist nor a fundamentalist. The following quotation from V. J. Bourke casts a good bit of light on the origins and method of "faith seeking understanding."

Actually the source of Augustine's views on faith and reason is a text from Isaias (7:9, Septuagint), which simply says: "Unless you will have believed, you will not understand" (*nisi credideritis non intelligetis*). The reading has been corrected in later texts ("if you will not believe, you shall not continue"), but this is a case of a fortunate error, more influential than the truth. From this misreading there developed a whole program of Christian intellectualism among the Latin Fathers of the Church and the theologians of the middle ages.[2]

In contemporary language we would more accurately call Augustine a theologian, that is, someone who uses reason to make clear the truth revealed by God. Augustine used this term to identify pagan writers on religion, like Porphyry. On the other hand, for Augustine, philosophy did not mean simply rational exploration of reality but what the term literally means—the love of wisdom. In *City of God* (8.8) Augustine applauds Plato for seeing that to philosophize is the same as to love God.[3] Augustine saw the work of philosophy as seeking, discovering, and intensely loving the final good of all human beings, the personal God who calls and enlightens all who find him. This definition is very far from a professional philosopher's idea, such as one might find in academia. The following quotation from the work contrasting the morals of the Manichees and the Christians gives a powerful picture of Augustine's idea of a person who truly is a philosopher.

The striving after God is therefore the desire of beatitude, the attainment of God is beatitude itself. We seek to attain God by loving Him; we attain to Him, not by becoming entirely what He is, but in nearness to Him, and in wonderful and sensible contact with Him, and in being inwardly illuminated and occupied by His truth and holiness. He is light itself; it is given to us to be illuminated by that light . . . since to seek the supreme good is to live well, that to live well is nothing else but to love God with all the heart, with all the soul, with all the mind; and, as arising from this, that this love be kept entire and incorrupt, which is the part of temperance; that it give way before no troubles, which is the part of fortitude; that it serve no other, which is the part of justice; that it be watchful in its discernment of things lest deception or fraud steal in, which is the part of prudence. This is man's one perfection, by which alone he can succeed in attaining to the purity of truth. (*De Moribus Ecclesiae* 1.11.19; 1.25.46)[4]

The reader sufficiently interested in this view of Augustine would do very well to study this question of reason and faith, of philosophy and the pursuit of wisdom, in the monumental work of Etienne Gilson, *The Christian Philosophy of St. Augustine.*[5]

Ironically, it is Augustine with his linking of reason and faith in the pursuit of philosophy (wisdom) who has a greater influence on modern philosophy than St. Thomas who, following Aristotle, constructs a worldview from reason alone and only when finished links this vision with the truths of faith. One of the profound insights of modern science, largely stemming from the theoretical constructs of Albert Einstein, is that one's assessment of any physical reality is affected by one's position in relationship to that reality. Augustine would certainly agree that our assessment of the human experience is deeply affected by our position as those with the gift of faith, so that the authority of the Divine Teacher may be said to enlighten the mind in its search for meaning.

Many readers are probably asking, Do you really mean to say

that the entire effort of secular learning, especially after the Enlightenment, which completely removes itself from revelation and faith, does not constitute a love of wisdom or true philosophy? Yes, that is exactly what St. Augustine would say. In fact, he even states that the true lover of wisdom cannot be a worldly man at all.

Whereas knowledge and action make a man happy, as in knowledge error must be guarded against, so must wickedness be avoided in action. Now whosoever supposes that he can know truth while he is still living iniquitously, is in error. And it is wickedness to love this world, and those things that come into being and pass away, and to lust after these things and to labour for them in order to acquire them, and to rejoice when they are abundant, and to fear lest they perish, and to be saddened when they perish. Such a life cannot see that pure, and undefiled, and immutable Truth, and cleave to it, to be for evermore unmoved. (*De Agone Christiano* 13.14)[6]

Many philosophers of the twentieth century, especially those called Existentialists, would agree with Augustine that if one believes in eternal beatitude one must use that belief in the construction of one's view of the meaning of life, one's real philosophy. Some of these philosophers might be of the opinion that there is no beatitude, that there is no God in the Judeo-Christian sense of a personal God who interacts with human beings. Well then, it is from this stance that they must make their search for the meaning of life, even if this opinion requires a rejection of all meaning. Augustine would have agreed with their assessment of things if he lacked faith as they do. But since he believes because of grace and knows by the authority of revelation that God seeks to draw him into a loving relationship this gives him a place of assessment of reality that must color all of his inquiry into the meaning of human existence. The reader might come to a better comprehension of faith-seeking-understanding as a philosophical stance by meditating on the following monumental prayer that Augustine includes in the *Soliloquies*. This work was written shortly after his conversion, while on a retreat at Cassiciacum with his mother and his friends. Using Augustine's *Against the*

Academics and his *Dialogue on the Blessed Life,* John J. O'Meara gives the following insights, which are helpful in understanding this prayer and the entire *Soliloquies.* "The influence of Neoplatonism . . . is seen here in the explanation of evil, in the sharp separation of sensible and intellectual perception and in the necessity of purification before one can know or ascend to God in elevation of the mind."[7]

In the beginning of the *Soliloquies* Augustine describes his state of mind in these terms. "I have been debating within myself many and diverse things seeking constantly and with anxiety to find out my real self, my best good, and the evil to be avoided. . . ."[8] In this frame of mind he composed this great meditation in the *Soliloquies,* which reads almost like a mantra.

The Soliloquies

O God, founder of the universe, help me, that, first of all, I may pray aright: and next, that I may act as one worthy to be heard by you: and finally, set me free.

God, through whom all things are, which of themselves could have no being; God, who does not permit that to perish, whose tendency it is to destroy itself! God, who has created out of nothing this world, which the eyes of all perceive to be most beautiful! God, who does not cause evil, but does cause that it shall not become the worst! God, who reveals to those few fleeing for refuge to that which truly is, that evil is nothing! God, through whom the universe, even with its perverse part, is perfect! God, to whom dissonance is nothing, since in the end the worst resolves into harmony with the better! God, whom every creature capable of loving, loves, whether consciously or unconsciously!

God, in whom all things are, yet whom the shame of no creature in the universe disgraces, nor his malice harms, nor his error misleads! God, who does not permit any save the pure to know the true! God, father of truth, father of wisdom, father of the true and perfect life, father of blessedness, father of the good and the beautiful, father of intelligible light, father of our awakening and enlightening, father of that pledge which warns us to return to you! . . .

God, whose gift it is that we do not utterly perish: God, by whom we are warned to watch: God, through whom we discriminate good things from evil things: God, through whom we flee from evil and follow after good: God, through whom we yield not to adversity: God, through whom we both serve well and rule well: God, through whom we discern that certain things we have deemed essential to ourselves are truly foreign to us, while those we had deemed foreign to us are essential: God, through whom we are not held fast by the baits and seduction of the wicked: God, through whom the decrease of our possessions does not diminish us: God, through whom our better part is not subject to our worse: God, through whom death is swallowed up in victory! God, who turns us about in the way: God, who strips us of that which is not, and clothes us with that which is: God, who makes us worthy of being heard: God, who defends us: God, who leads us into all truth: God, who speaks all good things to us: God, who does not deprive us of sanity nor permit another to do so: God, who recalls us to the path: God, who leads us to the door: God, who causes that it is open to those who knock: God, who gives us the bread of life: God, through whom we thirst for that water, which having drunk, we shall never thirst again: God, who convinces the world of the sin, of righteousness, and of judgment: God, through whom the unbelief of others does not move us: God, through whom we reprobate the error of those who deem that souls have no deserving in your sight: God, through whom we are not in bondage to weak and beggarly elements: God, who purifies and prepares us for diverse rewards, propitious, come to me!

In whatever I say come to my help, O you one God, one true eternal substance, where is no discord, no confusion, no change, no want, no death: where is all harmony, all illumination, all steadfastness, all abundance, all life: where nothing is lacking and nothing redundant: where begetter and begotten are one: God, whom all things serve which do serve and whom every good soul obeys.

At last I love you alone, you alone follow, you alone seek, you alone am I ready to serve: for you alone, by right, are ruler; under your rule do I wish to be. Command, I pray and order what you will, but heal and open my ears that I may hear your commands, heal and open my eyes that I may see your nod; cast all unsoundness from me that I may recognize you! Tell me whither to direct my gaze that I may look upon you, and I hope that I shall do all things which you command.

. . . Cause me, O father, to seek you; let me not stray from the path, and to me, seeking you, let nothing befall in place of yourself! If I desire nothing beside yourself, let me, I implore, find you now: but if there is in me the desire for something beside yourself, do you yourself purify me, and make me fit to look upon you! For the rest, whatever concerns the welfare of this mortal body of mine, so long as I do not know how it may serve either myself or those I love, to you, father, wisest and best, do I commit it, and I pray that you will admonish me concerning it as shall be needful. But this I do implore your most excellent mercy, that you convert me in my inmost self to you, and, as I incline toward you, let nothing oppose: and command that so long as I endure and care for this same body, I may be pure and magnanimous and just and prudent, a perfect lover and learner of your wisdom, a fit inhabitant of a dwelling place in your most blessed kingdom.

Amen and Amen![9]

This great prayer, one of the most powerful statements of theistic faith to be found outside the Scriptures, makes it clear that it would not have been possible for Augustine to put aside his faith for the sake of argument in order to convert the unbeliever. This technique (called theoretical atheism) starts out with the Christian philosopher or apologist saying: "All right, for the sake of argument we will say there is no God." St. Thomas does this in his polemical work *Summa Contra Gentiles*. To say that Augustine cannot do this and Thomas can is not to imply that the former is more devout than the latter but rather to present a somewhat different emphasis in both philosophy and epistemology, which is the study of how one comes to the knowledge of truth and to certitude. But before we read Augustine on such deep matters we must see where he gets his language.

What Words Mean to Augustine and Where He Gets Them

Vernon Burke sees the origins of Augustine's powerful use of words coming from three sources: (1) his training in Latin rhetoric (especially Virgil and Cicero); (2) his reading of Plato and the Neoplatonic writers who were influential in his youth (especially Plotinus and Porphyry); (3) and perhaps the greatest influence, his reading of the Scriptures in Latin. His incredible use of biblical sources give evidence of a mind steeped in both Old and New Testaments. This is all the more admirable when one remembers that it was Augustine's influence, especially at the Council of Carthage, that led to the codification of the New Testament as we now have it. A person familiar with the Bible and its use of words should be able to "read Augustine with understanding and enjoyment."[10]

A few descriptions of Augustine's favorite concepts are necessary. Reason (*ratio*) has two meanings in Augustine—the gaze of the mind, which can be turned toward all kinds of things simply by an act of the will; and also a superior reason when the mind is turned toward eternal unchangeable things. Most of our activities as human beings are involved with reason in the first meaning.

Knowledge pertains to things that are changeable, that is, not eternal or eternally true. Knowledge, although inferior to reason, is certainly necessary and helpful so long as it does not make a person proud. The love of eternal and unchangeable truth is what keeps knowledge from being a source of pride.[11] The life of virtue is impossible without knowledge—but wisdom, the contemplation of eternal truth, is the highest of all human experience.

Augustine the psychologist attempted an analysis of the sources and use of knowledge. The following quotation succinctly gives his analysis and illustrates Augustine's fascination with the phenomena of memory. Augustine also speaks here of true knowledge—which, according to him, contains the thing as it is true. Truth here means—as it does in most languages—an accurate agreement between a thought and the object that is thought about.

All these things, then, both those which the human mind knows by itself, and those which it knows by the bodily senses, and those which it has received and knows by the testimony of others, are laid up and retained in the storehouse of the memory; and from these is begotten a word that is true, when we speak what we know, but a word that is before all sound, before all thought of a sound. For the word is then most like to the thing known, from which also its image is begotten, since the sight of thinking arises from the sight of knowledge; when it is a word belonging to no tongue, but is a true word concerning a true thing, having nothing of its own, but wholly derived from that knowledge from which it is born. (*The Trinity* 15.12.22)[12]

More than anything else Augustine is interested in what is immediately true—that reality which goes beyond the senses and even the immutable mind itself. This possession of the immediately true is called wisdom or truth itself, far beyond the agreement of things with the mutable minds that grasp them using inferior knowledge.

It is very important for those reading Augustine as a spiritual writer to know what he means by truth. It is not merely, as we have said, the correspondence of thought and speech with extramental reality; truth can also mean the contemplation of immutable reality or eternal goodness.

No one can come to this truth without the unmerited gift of the grace of God. God's merciful love is absolutely essential for the contemplation of true wisdom. And the possibility of coming to the true wisdom is universal.

Therefore you must in no way deny that there is immutable truth which encompasses everything that is immutably true; you can not ascribe this truth to yourself or to me or to anyone because it is present to all and gives itself to all who discern things that are immutably true, like a light which in some marvelous way is both secret and yet available to all. . . . Look, Truth is in front of you— embrace it if you can and rejoice in it—and "delight in the Lord, and he will give you the desire of your heart" (Psalm 34). (*De Libro Arbitrio* 2.12.33)[13]

In the same book on free will Augustine induces another argument which appears incredibly to anticipate the knowledge of things which empirical psychology would discover sixteen hundred years later. He observes that we perceive things by what he calls rhythm and that things exist in a certain rhythmic pattern. When we perceive things with our senses we are not aware that we are really perceiving rhythmic impulses, but we perceive—as it were—a steady stream of data with no discreet phases or rhythm. The fact is that we actually perceive bits of data that come so quickly and rhythmically that they seem to be a steady flow of information. Sight illustrates this best. A young child and an older person (with a relatively slower perceptual mechanism) looking at a quickly flashing light will have a different experience. The child will see a flashing light and the older person will see a steady glow. The difference is called the critical flicker phenomenon. The child, in fact, is perceiving the reality of the light more accurately.

Along with this, most of the phenomena that we perceive are undulating: seasons, phases of heavenly bodies, the beating of the heart and pulse. Even the attempt to draw a straight line is done with undulation—a little in this direction and a little in the other. The following passage from his work on free will needs to be studied carefully not only because of the unusual argument it makes for the existence of God but also because it suggests that by the sincere pursuit of the author of reality one may come to a knowledge of wisdom.

Look at the sky and the earth and the sea, and everything that is observable in them or above them. They all have form because they have rhythm; take away rhythm and they will no longer be. From whom then do they proceed, except from Him from whom rhythm comes; since they exist only insofar as they are ordered by rhythm. . . . Go now to a place from which this rhythm proceeds, look for it and see if it exists in time and place; there will be no "when," there will be no "where" but rhythm exists, its limitation is not space nor is it measured in days or time. And yet when those who would be artists set themselves to learn their art they move in time and place, but their minds only exist in time since by the passage of time they may become more adept at art. Go beyond the mind of the artist so you may see the everlasting rhythm, then will wisdom shine upon you from her hiding place, from the very sanctuary of truth. (*De Libro Arbitrio* 16.42)[14]

Augustine goes on to say that if there were no rhythm in things they would fall into nothing. But we exist by measured motions and by a variety of forms, which like a poem must have an end. When we get to the end of things we ask: Where did all this form come from? Where did it begin? Augustine thought that it must be in the eternal and immutable form, which is neither contained in place or diffused in place, neither extended or varied in time, but through which all mutable things can receive a form and rhythm and accomplish their ordered purpose in time and place. In an incredible way Augustine seems to anticipate even the undulation theory of the creation of the cosmos. There are a number of present-day theories which hold that the cosmos is expanding but that eventually it will rhythmically contract in upon itself.

The modern reader is not used to such ideas as these. They are in fact quite Platonic. However, with a little effort one can begin to penetrate these ways of thinking which, to me, are often much more profound and revealing of truth than modern empiricism. This is not to say that empiricism does not have its place, but it is a rather narrow and myopic view of reality. Thinking and words like those given by Augustine in this discussion of rhythm and form are concepts that open to the human mind much greater vistas when we ask the question, "Where did this all come from and where is it going?"

The Origin and Love of Truth

There is nothing coldly intellectual and abstract about Augustine's love for truth. We who are familiar with modern philosophical ideas or even ideas drawn from religious apologetics like to see ourselves as being quite objective in our use of cool reason, as if this were ever completely possible. Augustine makes no pretense of this in his search for the truth. In his book *Against Lying* (*Contra Mendacium*), he writes: "What I put before the eyes of my heart (such as they are), the intellectual beauty of Him from whose mouth no false thing comes, though my weak and throbbing senses are driven back where truth in her radiance is more and more brightly shining upon me yet I am so inflamed with love for that surpassing beauty that I despise all human considerations which would call me back from pursuing it."[15]

Augustine's love for divine and immutable truth is passionate and deep. It also is based completely on Christian faith. Running through the writings of Augustine, one can hear the echoes of Paul's epistle to the Romans concerning the philosophers who do not know God—"God is true and every man is a liar" (Romans 3:4). In his sermon on Psalm 115 he writes:

Whatever man has in himself he is a liar, but by the grace of God he is made true. . . . Therefore it is most truly said that every man is a liar but God is true. But God is true when He said "you are gods, you are the sons of the most high, but you like all men shall die and shall fall like one of the princes" (Psalm 81:6). For if all men are liars they will not be liars insofar as they are no longer men. Since they shall be gods and sons of the Most High. O man, you are a liar by your own sin but you are true by the gift of God and no longer function as a mere man. (*Sermon on Psalm CXV* 3, 5)[16]

Saint Augustine powerfully and consistently taught that it required the grace of God through Christ to make a man a child of God. The modern reader again may have difficulty with this concept. It is, however, one that should be applied very easily to those who seek God with a sincere heart and have baptism of desire. In my own dealings with people who seek knowledge and others who seek wisdom I can easily single out those who have allowed themselves to be touched by grace and those who have not.

The latter may have a considerable amount of natural goodness about them, but they are not involved in truth; they are involved in knowledge. Perhaps the worst lies they tell, they tell to themselves. Inevitably, when I meet these people I come away with a prayer that since they are so close to seeking wisdom God will give them the grace to find it. On the other hand, one meets people who are somewhat lacking in natural abilities like intelli-

gence or even consistency, but by the grace of God they have some
knowledge of immutable truth. This indeed shows the mercy of
God. In *Sermon 166 on the New Testament,* St. Augustine writes:

The old man, that is, Adam, is concerned with lying; the new Man,
the Son of Man, that is Christ God, with truth. . . . If you would be
a man you will be a liar. Be not minded to be a man and you will
not be a liar. Put on Christ and you will be truthful; that the words
which you speak may not be yours, as if your own, and originated
by you but Truth's enlightening and illuminating you. For if you be
deprived of the light, you shall remain in your own darkness and
shall be able to speak nothing but lies. For the Lord himself says:
"He who speaks a lie, speaks of his own" (John viii,44), for every
"man is a liar" (Ps. cxv,II). Whoever therefore speaks the truth,
speaks not of his own but by God. (*Sermons on the New Testament* CLXVI, 2.2; 3.3)[17]

And thus Augustine as a philosopher cannot escape being at
the same time a theologian. Throughout the history of Western
philosophy and especially in the discussion of the writings of St.
Anselm, a disciple of St. Augustine, there has been a persistent
debate on whether one comes totally objectively to the knowledge of truth or whether one depends on some enlightenment
from above, or from some other source if a person is not a
believer. That source might even be one's own will. This argument rages, and we will not settle it here by any means. However,
let it be said for the reader of Augustine that he requires the grace
of God which comes ordinarily through deliberate and conscious
faith in Christ, although there is such a thing as baptism of desire
and union with Christ whom one does not clearly know.
Augustine maintains that this grace or goodness of God is absolutely necessary to come to perennial and eternal wisdom. You
cannot read Augustine well if you do not understand that.

Augustine as Psychologist

St. Augustine is often referred to as "the holy psychologist," and
indeed he was both a saint and a profound student of human
behavior. We have already seen that the *Confessions* is, by a thou-

sand years, the first psychological autobiography. In the history of psychology Augustine is credited with raising many of the serious questions with which contemporary behavioral sciences are concerned. We need also to remember that he was very much a pioneer, as were the classical and patristic Greek writers. These include thinkers as different as Democratus with his four temperaments and St. Gregory of Nyssa with his insight about developmental levels of the spiritual life. Like all explorers, Augustine and those before him developed maps of human behavior which are not relevant to our time and culture and yet which possess a perennial value.

The two most interesting psychological questions for those interested in Augustine as a spiritual writer are his concept of the inner person and the idea of free will. We will briefly try to sum up these two questions in a way that will assist the reader.

The Inner Person

The Bible itself often speaks of the inner person or nature, contrasting it to the outer person or nature. In older translations the phrase used was "inner and outer man"; among familiar examples are St. Paul's use of this idea in Romans 7:23 and 2 Corinthian 4:16. In contemporary translations the use of these terms is dropped so as to avoid any appearance of dualism. In fact, the older translations are more faithful to the Greek.

St. Augustine was emphatically not a philosophical dualist, that is, a person who believes in two equal governing principles of reality, one good and the other evil. He had rejected the dualism of the Manicheans even before his conversion to Christ. Psychological dualism is another thing. In its more palatable form it might use the analogy of Descartes, who described the human being as an angel using a machine.

In a perceptive article on the "inner man" of St. Augustine, Gareth B. Matthews summarizes the very frequent use of this metaphor by the great fourth-century psychologist.

> Typically Augustine speaks of remembering, imaging, visualizing, conceiving, and understanding as cases of seeing something with the inner eye. He describes what a man is thinking on a par-

ticular occasion, as well as the intention he forms to do something, as the speech of an inner voice, or equivalently, as what a man says in his heart. He conceives the desire to do something as doing it already in one's heart. And he distinguishes the man who acts with a pure motive from his Pharisaical neighbor by saying that, though both, for example, give alms outwardly, only the man of pure motive also gives alms inwardly. In short, the family of inner man locutions provides for Augustine a connected way of conceiving mental functions and narrating psychological episodes.[18]

After a thorough study, Matthews concludes that Augustine is not a philosophical dualist but one who employs a familiar biblical usage found occasionally in the New Testament (especially in St. Paul) but even in the Jewish Scriptures, as well as in early Christian writings. We find this usage even in the words of our Lord in the Sermon on the Mount when he speaks of someone committing adultery in his heart (Matthew 5:27).

Augustine often employs such biblical usage, but when confronted with philosophical dualism he clearly maintains the traditional Christian position of the unity of the whole human being. The following text from *City of God* makes Augustine's thinking very clear:

A man is not just a body, or just a soul, but a being made up of both body and soul. . . . The soul is not the whole man, but the better part of a man. *When both are joined together they have the name "man," which, however, they do not either one lose when we speak of them singly.* For who is prohibited from saying, in ordinary language, "That man is dead and is now in peace or in torment," though this can be said only of the soul; or "That man is buried in that place or in that," though this cannot be understood except as referring to the body alone? Will they say that Holy Scripture follows no such usage? On the contrary it so thoroughly adopts it, that even when a man is alive, and his body and soul are joined together, it calls each of them singly by the name "man," speaking of the soul as the "inner man" and the body as the "outer man," as if there were two men, although both together are one man. (*City of God* 12.24,2)[19]

It is clear from this quotation that Augustine does not see the inner and outward man as two separate beings or two separate "supposites," that is two separate ultimate subjects of predication. Quite the opposite, the inner and outer man share moral responsibility together and often have to struggle with this. There is no indication that when St. Paul uses "inner and outward man" he is really suggesting an absolute dualism.

Matthew concludes that Augustine culled these ways of speaking of the inward and outward man from the Bible and that he does not intend to establish something like a Cartesian dualism at all. This is apparent from many passages where he writes definitively on the subject of the unity of the human person. It is worth mentioning that there are those in our time who accuse Augustine of psychological dualism but would never think of making the same accusation against Freud with his inner troika of id, ego, and superego or against Jung with the various inner structures he suggests within the mind.

What Augustine has done by bringing these biblical images of inner and outer man into the thought of Western civilization has been to open the doors to a more profound and enriched analogy of the complexity of human cognition and self-direction. Modern psychology would be a very sparse landscape indeed if psychologists did not have an ability to describe various phases of human activity as if they were somewhat autonomous. Such expressions of Augustine as inner speaking or inner smiling, or the eyes of the heart enrich the rhetoric with which we can discuss the complexity of human experience. This experience is made up not only of a rich perceptual panorama but of a much more complex inner dynamism which all comes mysteriously together in the phenomenal ego, the marvelously mysterious person I call "myself."

Free to Do and Free to Do Good

If we return to the analogy of the Augustinian Alps, we are about to enter the deepest valley, one so deep that it almost looks like a well where it is possible to see the stars overhead even during daylight. Without writing a heavy tome but simply a guide book

for spiritual reading, I am faced with the difficult task of introducing you to the thorniest question Augustine ever took up.
Augustine bravely faced the questions of human freedom, of
original sin, which we inherit, and actual sin, which is committed
by the best of us. The perplexing question of God's foreknowledge of our individual acts and of our particular eternal destinies,
salvation or eternal loss, ultimately is shrouded in the mystery of
time and eternity. The very greatest theologians who have taken
Augustine as their guide through these mysterious questions
have come up with answers as different as those of Thomas
Aquinas and John Calvin. We are not going to answer these questions, or even adequately describe them. But in our explanation
we must at least acknowledge the existence of the question and
try to have some notion of Augustine's answers.[20]

There is fairly general agreement that for Augustine the
human psyche (or mind) was a moral agent; humans unlike animals are responsible for what they do. Rist points out:

> Thus *voluntas* (will) is not a decision making faculty of the indi-
> vidual as subsequent philosophers might lead us to suppose but
> the individual himself.[21]

Citing Luke 2:14, St. Augustine identifies good people as
people of good will—not *with* good wills. Thus, some people are
good because they desire the good, and others are bad because
they desire either evil or the absence of good or a lesser good. If a
person is compelled to do something by external force, according
to Augustine that person really does not do it. Otherwise, one is
free to do good or evil. Thus, Augustine would not seem to be
able to take into account psychological compulsion. He often
used the idea of concupiscence and its power over the individual,
but it would be many centuries before those who think about
human behavior would be able to deal with the concept of compulsion as something that diminishes one's responsibility. In our
own time we take for granted that compulsion reduces responsibility, and perhaps we err occasionally and become enablers of
evil deeds. In the *Confessions,* Augustine recounts in many places
how his own sinful behavior was occasioned by the bad example
of the whole society around him, and he sees himself as more or
less responsible; but he also sees God as having mercy on him.

This implies that at least he sees himself as much a victim as a sinner.

O God, my God, what emptiness and mockeries did I now experience: for it was impressed upon me as right and proper in a boy to obey those who taught me, that I might get on in the world and excel in the handling of words to gain honour among men and deceitful riches. I, poor wretch, could not see the use of the things I was sent to school to learn; but if I proved idle in learning, I was soundly beaten. For this procedure seemed wise to our ancestors: and many, passing the same way in the days past, had built a sorrowful road by which we too must go, with multiplication of grief and toil upon the sons of Adam.

Yet in acting against the commands of my parents and schoolmasters, I did wrong, O Lord my God, Creator and Ruler of all things, but of sin not Creator but Ruler only: for I might later have made good use of those lessons that they wanted me to learn, whatever may have been their motive in wanting it. I disobeyed, not because I had chosen better, but through sheer love of play: I loved the vanity of victory, and I loved too to have my ears tickled with the fictions of the theatre which set them to itching ever more burningly: and in my eyes a similar curiosity burned increasingly for the games and shows of my elders. (*Conf.* 1.9)[22]

In this quotation the very important distinction of St. Augustine about freedom becomes clear: the freedom to act, the freedom to do good. Augustine sees himself as responsible for his behavior as a child, his freedom to chose to learn or to play. But he prays for greater freedom for himself and all others. What is this freedom? It is the freedom to do good which we call grace and which is given to human beings only by the mercy or goodness of God. It is a basic principle of Western philosophy, both classical and scholastic, that the human will can be drawn only to what is perceived to be good. When a person willfully does evil, it is because he sees it as a good and allows himself to be deceived. Psychologically, the act of sin is rooted in the willingness or the necessity of being deceived. The human being bound by cupidity or concupiscence and deception, left to his or her own devices in this fallen world, will choose evil or a lesser good than the one for which we were created—the blessed possession of God.

In Augustine's eyes, we human beings are so fallen that we cannot lift ourselves up; we cannot turn to the consistent pursuit of our transcendent eternal goal, that is, union with God. It would be wrong to think that Augustine sees all unredeemed human beings always choosing evil. In *City of God*, he acknowledges the natural virtues and good qualities of the early founders of Rome.[23] In fact his argument is that those natural virtues gave Rome its early glory, and the loss of these virtues has led to its decline.

One must never lose sight of Augustine's profound recognition of the pervasive effects of original sin and his view that the situation of human beings now is very different from that of either the angels or the first parents before the fall. He makes grace, which is won for all by Christ, the unique and single force that can bring the lives of human beings to a point where they are capable of doing any good that has everlasting consequences—that is, beatitude in the world to come. He makes this pointedly clear: "Carnal cupidity reigns when the charity of God is not found."[24]

The following quotation from John Rist makes Augustine's point very clear:

> In brief, when Augustine says that our choices are free, he does not mean that we are autonomous beings, able to weigh up good and evil courses of action and decide upon the one or the other. Unless he is helped by God's grace, fallen man's freedom of choice is only the freedom to sin. We are free and able to do evil of our own accord, but we are unable to choose the good freely. In short, when Augustine says that fallen man is free and has free choices, he means that he is free from virtue and the slave of vice, free from one kind of love, that is, devoid of *caritas*, but the servant of its opposite, namely *cupiditas*. Man belongs to one of two camps and obeys one of two rulers. Freedom is obedience to God, the choice and performance of good works under the guidance of God's grace. It is freedom from the necessity of sin. Thus we are brought to the view that, although our "wills" and our "choices" are free, in the sense that we alone are responsible for them, yet without the intervention of God we are bound to an evil which we cannot escape.[25]

The reader, perhaps regrettably unfamiliar with the Catholic doctrine of original sin, may find this teaching "pessimistic," as some who ought to know better have characterized it. Why should we be held responsible for a sin committed eons ago by the first members of our race? Why should all this misery, much of it caused by human sinfulness, be heaped upon us innocent creatures of this enlightened age? Augustine starts with the obvious fact, observable by any thinking person, that there is something very wrong with the world and with our own selves. This fact is inescapable but equally mysterious. The simple answer is we do not understand why a world so beautiful can be so dangerous and ugly, but it is. Augustine seeks the answer in biblical revelation, having spent the first decades of his vibrant life trying to find this answer in cults and philosophy. The partial answer to the problem of being evil is to be found in the solidarity of the human race with our first parents. We inherit great blessings from these first parents: sight, hearing, the ability to walk, and especially the capacity to think, decide, and love. Why can't we also inherit their wounds? Is this so improbable, seeing that no one else has any answers at all to the question of why evil exists in the world? Augustine states this doctrine clearly.

God, the Author of all natures but not of their defects, created man good; but man, corrupted by choice and condemned by justice, has produced a progeny that is both corrupt and condemned. For, we all existed in that one man, since, taken together we were the one man who fell into sin through the woman who was made out of him before sin existed. Although the specific form by which each of us was to live was not yet created and assigned, our nature was already present in the seed from which we were to spring. And because this nature has been soiled by sin and doomed to death and justly condemned, no man was to be born of man in any other condition.

Thus, from a bad use of free choice, a sequence of misfortunes conducts the whole human race, excepting those redeemed by the grace of God, from the original canker in its root to the devastation of a second and endless death. (*City of God* 13.14)

Augustine is rightly called the Doctor of grace and not the

Doctor of sin. In innumerable passages he praises and glorifies God for his many mercies on the human race and the individual. One can never appreciate St. Augustine, or in my opinion St. Paul, unless one understands the necessity of grace for us to perform acts that contribute to our eternal destiny. The following quotation from the *Exposition on the Psalms* makes very clear the distinction between being free (to sin) and freed (to do good).

Let man choose for himself what he will; the works of the Lord are not so constituted that the creature, constituted with a free will, should transcend the will of the Creator, even though he act contrary to His will. For God wills not that you should sin, since He forbids it. Yet if you sinned, do not think a man has done what he willed, and that that has happened to God which He did not will. For as He wills that man should not sin, so will He spare the sinner, that he may return and live. So too is it His will finally to punish one who persists in his sin, that the rebellious may not escape the power of justice. Thus whatever choice you make, the Almighty will not be at a loss to fulfil His will concerning you. (*Exposition on the Psalms* 110.2)[26]

Modern readers, understandably, have difficulty with the idea of God being in any way responsible for the loss of a soul. Usually in such discussions, the whole profound mystery of the divine will as well as the mystery of human freedom and God's foreknowledge of our individual destinies is ignored. People want easy answers. And in good times it is easy to say that everybody means well and is going to go to heaven. However, when people live in times of brutality, sadism, and genocide, those facile answers give way to consideration of God's justice because there is little justice in the world. Some, then, think of eternal loss as a sublimation of their own feelings of vengeance against their enemies.

Others, more thoughtfully, ponder the meaning of sinful acts, horrendous deeds, and the obvious freedom with which they are done. Augustine lived at times when the Roman Empire was quite capable of great cruelty, and the barbarians were descending on the civilized world with wanton brutality and horror. The children of our century, if they are wise and have the intellectual fortitude to do so, should ponder the brutality of the twentieth century from holocaust to genocide before they read the following text. Yes, Augustine believed in the existence of hell, the dreadful loss of eternal destiny. So did all of the New Testament writers. Christ warned the people of this dreadful possibility over and over again in the parables and in all his preaching.

The question is, "Does the merciful God send the lost souls to hell?" Augustine's answer is that they send themselves and that they even make the hell that they find. This theme—hell being the creation of the lost—is one that would be developed later by the medieval mystics. Augustine states his case so well in the following quotation from the *Exposition on the Psalms* that as I read it, I recall my own horror on leaving the Dachau concentration camp museum when I saw a picture of the SS guards having a beer party. Under the picture was the question: "Where are they now?"

When God punishes sinners, He does not inflict His evil on them, but leaves them to their own evil. "Behold," says the Psalmist, "he has been in labour with injustice, he has conceived toil; brought forth iniquity. He has opened a pit and dug it: and he is fallen into the hole he made. His sorrow shall be turned on his own head: and his iniquity shall come down upon his crown." (Ps. viii,15) When therefore God punishes, He punishes as a judge those that transgress the law, not by bringing evil upon them from Himself, but by driving them on to that which they have chosen, to fill up the sum of their misery. (*Exposition on the Psalms* 5.10)[27]

The question of salvation is deeply imbedded in all of Augustine's thinking about the human mind because unlike modern writers, he would not and could not distinguish between a well-ordered life and a life ordered toward God. If you were going to talk to Augustine about the universal human goal of happiness, you had to be speaking about a happiness that time could not carry away.

This became all the more clear in the writings of Augustine as he became an old man. He lived twenty years after the sack of Rome by Alaric, years in which it became more and more apparent that the Roman civilization was in decline and could not defend itself from the barbarians. During the last decade of

Augustine's life the prosperous Roman colonial civilization in North Africa was threatened and then devastated. Hippo, his home and diocese, was attacked, pillaged, and partially burned in the year after Augustine's death. (His library was almost miraculously spared and moved to safety.)[28] During his last decade as bishop, life was a daily round of caring for refugees, of hearing stories of horror, of watching helplessly as civilization gave place to wanton ruin. Eventually, the barbarians set up kingdoms and settled down, but they did not do this in Africa. Peter Brown sums up this dramatic moment, describing eloquently Augustine as he lived through and died in this apocalyptic time.

> An ancient terror had suddenly come back to these civilized bishops: fear of the wholesale lapse of the faithful under persecution, fear of massacre, of subtle propaganda, of ingenious torture. Augustine had ordered the bishops to stay by their flocks: as the Vandals closed in around Hippo, he would pray that he and his congregation might be able to persevere through what lay ahead.
>
> The "gift of perseverance," he had said, was the greatest of God's gifts to the individual. For it bestowed on frail human beings the same unshakable stability as the human nature in Christ had enjoyed: by this gift, a man was joined forever to the Divine, could be confident that the "hand of God" would be stretched above him to shield him, unfailingly, against the world. "Human nature could not have been raised higher."
>
> But the elect received this gift so that they, also, could tread the hard way of Christ. It was for this that they needed "a liberty . . . protected and made firm by the gift of perseverance, that this world should be overcome, the world, that is, in all its deep loves, in all its terrors, in all its countless ways of going wrong."[29]

It is on this dramatic note that we draw to an end our consideration of Augustine as a psychologist. He is preeminently a believing psychologist or, to use a phrase popular now, "a Christian psychologist." He cannot be understood outside the context of faith because, to use his own phrase, he sees all human beings as "restless until they rest" in God. The question of predestination is still something of a mystery. For those concerned to understand Augustine's thinking on this mystery, I would be bold enough to state the following summary of his thought: God offers his mercy to those who do not deserve it so that they may be saved. They must do their part to receive it and work with grace by following the gospel. God does not cause people to be lost. His mercy is infinite but coexists with his justice. Augustine often prays for his own enemies, for those who seem to be lost; and he is deeply concerned about infants and children, especially the innocent victims of cruelty and war and those who die without baptism.

Perhaps the greatest difference between Augustine's thinking and our own is that we have a deeper appreciation of how much human responsibility is diminished by psychological compulsion and the effects of culture. We hope we are correct in seeing the mercy of God extending beyond those who struggle to follow the Christian life. But Augustine, too, had a sense of God's mercy to the lost sheep. After all, he had been one of them.

As regards the final outcome of the drama of salvation, we offer the following selection from *Exposition on the Psalms* 36:

And their inheritance shall be forever. This we take on faith. Does the Lord also take it on faith? The Lord knows these things with a clarity so distinct that it is beyond our reach to describe, even when we are made equal to the angels. For the things to be revealed will not show forth as plainly to us as they show forth to Him who is incapable of change. Yet what are we told even of ourselves? *Dearly beloved, we are now the sons of God and it hath not yet appeared what we shall be. We know that, when He shall appear, we shall be like to Him, because we shall see Him as He is.* [1 John 3:2] There is obviously, then, some kind of blissful vision reserved for us; and if at present only a partial glimpse may be caught *through a glass in a dark manner,* [1 Cor. 13:12] yet the radiant beauty of that beatitude which God stores up for them that fear Him, which He perfects for them that hope in Him, utterly transcends the power of speech. It is for this that our hearts are being trained in all the hardships and trials of this life. Do not feel surprise at being schooled amid toil: you are being schooled for a wondrous destiny.[30]

✚ Chapter Three ✚

Augustine—
The Preacher of the Word

What would the Alps be without the spectacular green valleys, dotted with towns and villages, filled with pastures and speckled with wildflowers and gardens? They would be a lot of forbidding rocks, a no man's land. It is the deep and fertile valleys with lakes and streams fed from the high peaks above that make the mountains all the more beautiful. The fields and valleys of the Augustinian panorama are the more than eight hundred sermons, homilies, and commentaries that he wrote in his years as bishop of Hippo.

We will find some rest and respite after our climb on the peaks and cliffs of philosophy and psychology by strolling through the vast valleys of these easier readings. Take time to enjoy these valleys because there are high peaks ahead.

Parenthetically, I should mention at this point that along with his homilies Augustine wrote over four hundred letters, some of them small books, on an immense number of theological and spiritual topics. He found time to compose smaller books as widely ranging as the *Greatness of the Human Soul*, *The Christian Combat*, *On Lying*, and *On the Happy Life*. An alphabetical list of his writings can be found in *The Essential Augustine*, edited by Vernon J. Bourke.[1]

Bourke also conveniently gives English translations where available and a list of the original and standard sources which are usually named by initials that leave the beginner mystified. For instance, PL means Patrologia Latina edited by J. P. Minge in the mid-nineteenth century. This series in Latin and PG (Patrologia Graeca) in Greek are to be found in good libraries of seminaries and universities. FOC (Fathers of the Church) and ACW (Ancient Christian Writers) are two sets of English translations done in the United States in recent decades. ACW has eight volumes on Augustine, and FOC has sixteen volumes.

You may recall that we mentioned smaller and more recent collections in the introduction, especially the very tangy and up-to-date translation of Fr. Edmund Hill, O.P., and the beautiful and flowing version of Sr. Mary Clark. There are also special selections of Augustine's sermons in the four volumes of the Liturgy of the Hours. In fact, ninety-three passages can be read during the entire liturgical year.

As I mentioned, when I surveyed the voluminous writings of St. Augustine I felt like a tour guide in the Alps trying to decide what valleys and lakes to explore with visitors whose time was limited indeed. You will realize my dilemma when I tell you I spent an hour most afternoons for eight years in the seminary reading the Oxford translations of the *Sermons and Homilies on St. John and on the Psalms.* I owe what sanity survived the rigors of the old seminary to St. Augustine, Dostoyevsky, and Guardini. How can I arrange all of this, I asked, and an answer came as I prayed the daily readings. St. Augustine practically always wrote about one theme—Christ. When we call him the preacher of the word we don't mean the Bible as the Word of God, but the Eternal Word, the Logos, made flesh and dwelling among us, crucified, risen, and coming again. The life of our Lord himself gives the perfect framework for which selections to include from this great wealth of material—and much of the selection process has been done by scholars who have already chosen the most meaningful passages. What tour guide has failed to learn from the guides who went before him? We will try as best we can to date the works cited, but these dates are not always precise and the theories on dating are not always available. There is one serious warning. A selection may leave you with the impression that you have read it all, like those dangerous recordings of "The Best of Bach" or guide books offering "Highlights of the Louvre." This introductory selection is meant to lead you into a good library or competent bookstore so you can really get started.

The Coming of the Savior

Christ came to the young Augustine not in Galilee but in Tagaste and Carthage, in Rome and Milan, as he struggled to find meaning and truth, self control and human dignity in the conflict with his vices. Christ was in every way a Savior for this troubled and brilliant young man. I suspect that every year as Advent rolled around Augustine, like so many adult converts, rejoiced again in the coming of the Lord. The following sermon (185), taken from the Liturgy of the Hours for Christmas Eve, gives one a moving experience of what Christ meant to the bishop many years after his own conversion.[2]

Awake, mankind! For your sake God has become man. *Awake, you who sleep, rise up from the dead, and Christ will enlighten you.* I tell you again: for your sake, God became man.

You would have suffered eternal death, had he not been born in time. Never would you have been freed from sinful flesh, had he not taken on Himself the likeness of sinful flesh. You would have suffered everlasting unhappiness, had it not been for this mercy. You would never have returned to life, had He not shared your death. You would have been lost if he had not hastened to your aid. You would have perished, had he not come.

Let us then joyfully celebrate the coming of our salvation and redemption. Let us celebrate the festive day on which he who is the great and eternal day came from the great and endless day of eternity into our own short day of time.

He has become our justice, our sanctification, our redemption, so that, as it is written: Let him who glories glory in the Lord.

Justified by faith, let us be at peace with God: for justice and peace have embraced one another. Through our Lord Jesus Christ: for Truth has arisen from the earth. Through whom we have access to that grace in which we stand, and our boast is in our hope of God's glory. He does not say: "of our glory," but *of God's glory:* for *justice* has not proceeded from us but has *looked down from heaven.* Therefore *he who glories, let him glory,* not in himself, but *in the Lord. . . .*

For this reason, when our Lord was born of the Virgin, the message of the angelic voices was: *Glory to God in the highest, and peace to his people on earth.*

For how could there be peace of earth unless *Truth has arisen from the earth,* that is, unless Christ were born of our flesh? And *he is our peace who made the two into one:* that we might be men of good will, sweetly linked by the bond of unity.

In this citation we have a succinct but absolutely clear confession of the divinity of Christ, salvation through the incarnation and suffering of the Messiah.

The God-Man

Augustine was a great Scripture scholar and was especially expert on the book of Genesis and the Johannine and Pauline writings. That the only Son of God had become a human being so that human beings could enter into the divine promises of eternal life was a mystery that overwhelmed him with gratitude. The God-man became poor, that we could become rich in the treasures of wisdom and knowledge. The theme of desire for these treasures, so familiar from the *Confessions,* runs through this Christmas sermon (194) so clearly that I think if I found it unsigned I would know immediately that it was written by the Bishop of Hippo.

What man knows all the treasures of wisdom and knowledge hidden in Christ, concealed in the poverty of his flesh? Scripture says: *Although he was rich he became poor for our sake to enrich us by his poverty.* He showed Himself poor when He assumed our mortal nature and destroyed death, yet He promised us riches, for He had not been robbed of His wealth but was keeping it in reserve.

How great are the blessings of His goodness which He reserves for those who fear Him and shows to those who hope in Him! Until

He gives them to us in their plenitude, we can have only the faintest conception of them; but to enable us to receive these blessings, He who in His divine nature is the equal of the Father assumed the condition of a slave and became like us, and so restored to us our likeness to God. The only Son of God became a son of man to make many men sons of God. He instructed slaves by showing Himself in the form of a slave, and now He enables free men to see him in the form of God.

For *we are the sons of God, and although what we shall be has not yet been revealed, we know that when He appears we shall be like Him for we shall see Him as He is.* For what are those treasures of wisdom and knowledge, what those divine riches, if not the one thing that can fulfill our longing? What are the great blessings of his goodness, if not the one thing that will content us? Therefore: *Show us the Father, and all our desires will be satisfied.*

Since we can as yet form no conception of His generation by the Father before the daystar, let us keep the festival of His birth of a virgin in the hours of the night. Since it is still beyond our understanding that *His name endures for ever and existed before the sun,* let us at least recognize *His dwelling* that he has placed beneath the sun. We cannot yet behold Him as the only Son, abiding for ever in His Father, so let us recall *His coming forth like a bridegroom from his chamber.* We are not yet ready for the banquet of our Father, so let us contemplate the manger of Jesus Christ our Lord.[3]

Augustine loved paradox, the resolution of mystery by the statement of correlative mysteries and apparently contradictory realities. The expression "God-man" is in itself the origin of a string of paradoxes. The following quotation from another Christmas sermon (184) demonstrates the use of paradox so characteristic of the great preacher bishop.

By His birth of an earthborn mother He hallowed this one day who by His birth of the Father was the Creator of all ages. In the one birth a mother was impossible, while for the other no human father was required. In fact, Christ was born both of a father and of a mother, both without a father and without a mother; of a father as

God, of a mother as man; without a mother as God, without a father as man. *Who,* then, *shall declare His generation?* The one is without time, the other without parallel; the one which has always been, the other which has never been before or since—

Rightly, therefore, did the Prophets announce that He was to be born, and the heavens and the angels that He had been born. He whose hands governed the world, lay in the manger; and Infant that He was, He was also the Word. Him whom the heavens cannot contain, the womb of one woman bore. She ruled our Ruler; she carried Him in whom we are; she gave milk to our Bread.

O manifest infirmity, O wondrous humility, in which all the greatness of God lay hid![4]

Christ came to teach and to fashion his disciples into a church, which at that time they did not know was to be his mystical body. They would mysteriously become members of him because this is the way of salvation. In the next selections we will ponder Augustine's thought on the teachings Christ gave in his public life.

Follow Me

What does it mean to follow Christ? And who is called to follow? Augustine preached in a time of new converts, when there was confusion and strife among Christians and the constant harassment of the still active pagan world. We live in times that are similar, and I have found this sermon (96) to be most enlightening about the Christian life.

If anyone wishes to come after me, let him deny himself, take up his cross and follow me. The Lord's command seems difficult and painful: that anyone who wishes to follow him must deny himself. But His command is not really difficult or painful, since He Himself helps us to do what He commands. For the verse of the psalm addressed to Him was truly spoken: *Because of the words of your lips I have abided by hard ways.* True also are His own words: *My yoke is mild and my burden is light.* For love makes easy whatever is difficult in His commands.

What does it mean, *let him take up his own cross?* It means he must endure many things that are painful; that is the way he must follow Me. When he begins to follow Me in My life and My teachings, many will contradict him, try to stop him, or dissuade him, even those who call themselves Christ's disciples. It was they who walked with Christ that tried to stop the blind men from calling out to Him. So if you wish to follow Christ, you will take these threats or flattery or any kind of obstacle and fashion them into the cross; you must endure it, carry it, and not give way under it. And so in this world that is the Church, a world of the good, the reconciled, and the saved—or rather, those destined for salvation, but already saved by hope, as it is written, *by hope we are saved*—in this world of the Church, which completely follows Christ, he has said to everyone: *If anyone wishes to follow me, let him deny himself.*

This is not a command for virgins to obey and brides to ignore, for widows and not for married women, for monks and not for married men, or for the clergy and not for the laity. No, the whole Church, the entire body, all the members in their distinct and varied functions, must follow Christ. She who is totally unique, the dove, the spouse who was redeemed and dowered by the blood of her bridegroom is to follow him. There is a place in the Church for the chastity of the virgin, for the continence of the widow, and for the modesty of the married. Indeed, all her members have their place, and this is where they are to follow Christ, in their function and in their way of life. They must deny themselves, that is, they must not presume on their own strength. They must take up their cross by enduring in the world for Christ's sake whatever pain the world brings.[5]

Ascend in the Heart

A number of Augustine's sermons are instructions to the newly baptized, encouraging them in the Christian life. These are remarkably beautiful instructions because they assume that the recent converts from paganism are enthusiastic about growing spiritually. Certain psalms were considered most appropriate for these converts. They are called in Scripture "The Songs of Ascents," and in the present enumeration they include Psalms 120 to 134; in the liturgy they are called "The Gradual Psalms." *Gradus* means "ascent." In the old enumeration they began with Psalm 119, which is now called Psalm 120. Sister Clarke provides a commentary and sensitive translation of the homilies on these psalms. Augustine uses the word "ascents" to develop the whole idea of the spiritual life as rising to God made possible by the descent of Christ into this valley of tears. Christ, therefore, not only saves us by his suffering but gives us an example of how we must live so as to rise toward God.

Where then are these ascents? In the heart. What more shall I say to you that this man (the Psalmist) in whom speaks the Holy Spirit has said to us? Is it to this place or to another? Whatever I say, you imagine some earthly place, crawling on the ground, weighed down by the flesh, the soul burdened by the corruptible body, this earthly dwelling place beating down the mind capable of the highest thoughts (Wis 9:15). To whom shall I say it? Who will hear? Who will understand where we shall be in the afterlife if we ascend in heart? Since no one can understand it, let us hope for an ineffable realm of bliss which He who has set stops of ascent in your heart has prepared for you. But where? In the valley of tears. A valley is a symbol of humility as the mountain is the symbol of loftiness. The mountain which we must ascend is a kind of spiritual loftiness. And what is this mountain which we must ascend if not Our Lord Jesus Christ? It is He who, by His sufferings, has made for us a valley of tears, as He has made by His abiding a mountain of ascent. What is a valley of tears? "The Word was made flesh and dwelt among us" (Jn 1:14). What is a valley of tears? He has turned His cheek to those who would strike Him and was covered with opprobrium (Lam 3:30). What is a valley of tears? He was scourged, covered with spittle, crowned with thorns, nailed to the cross. From this valley of tears you must ascend. But ascend where? "In the beginning was the Word, and the Word was with God, and the Word was God" (Jn 1:1). For He Himself, the "Word was made flesh and dwelt among us." Abiding in Himself, He descended to you. He descended to you so as to become for you a valley of tears; He abode in Himself so as to be for you a mountain of ascent.

Let us sing, then, my Brothers, this "Song of Steps," resolved to ascend in heart; for Christ descended to us so that we might ascend. Jacob saw a ladder, and on this ladder he saw some ascending, others descending (Gn 28:12); he saw both. In those who ascended we can recognize those who progressed in piety: and in those who descended those who lagged behind. This is in fact what we find among the People of God. Some progress, others remain behind. Such is perhaps the meaning of the ladder.[6]

Later in the final chapter when we consider Augustine as a spiritual guide, we will return to these psalms and many specific lessons drawn from the preaching of our Savior during his earthly life. Now we must turn our attention to one of Augustine's most important and central contributions, the development of the doctrine of the Mystical Body of Christ. You must have an appreciation of this teaching before we can adequately consider the culmination of Christ's life in the mysteries of Holy Week.

Christ, Our Head

Our salvation, according to Augustine, completely depends on the "mediator between God and men, the man Christ Jesus, who is over all things, God blessed forever, who is calling to me and saying, 'I am the Way, the Truth and the Life'" (*Confessions* 7.18). The *Homilies on St. John* are filled with teachings about Christ our Mediator and the Head of the church. Doctor Bernard McGinn, whose work we shall engage later in the chapter on Augustine the mystic, puts it succinctly when he says: "It would be hard to exaggerate the emphasis that Augustine placed on the doctrine of the Body of Christ."[7] McGinn gives a clear statement of this doctrine, which is often described in rather obscure terms: "The unity between Christ and his Body means that by our membership in the church we share in all the *magnalia Christi,* the great mysteries by which the God-man wrought our redemption. This is an ontological bond, a real participation in his life, and not just some

form of moral imitation of Christ's good example."[8] The following passage from the *Commentary on Psalm 85* is the second reading for Wednesday of the fifth week of Lent. Outside the New
Testament itself, I think it would be difficult to find a clearer and
more sublime statement of this fundamental Christian belief.

God could give no greater gift to men than to make his Word,
through whom he created all things, their head and to join them to
him as his members, so that the Word might be both Son of God
and son of man, one God with the Father, and one man with all
men. The result is that when we speak with God in prayer we do
not separate the Son from him, and when the body of the Son
prays it does not separate its head from itself: it is the one Savior
of his body, our Lord Jesus Christ, the Son of God, who prays for
us and in us and is himself the object of our prayers.

He prays for us as our priest, he prays in us as our head, he is the
object of our prayers as our God.

Let us then recognize both our voice in his, and his voice in ours.
When something is said, especially in prophecy, about the Lord
Jesus Christ that seems to belong to a condition of lowliness
unworthy of God, we must not hesitate to ascribe this condition to
one who did not hesitate to unite himself with us. Every creature
is his servant, for it was through him that every creature came to
be. . . .

Yet in other parts of Scripture we hear him as one sighing, praying, giving praise and thanks. We hesitate to attribute these
words to him because our minds are slow to come down to his
humble level when we have just been contemplating him in his
divinity. It is as though we are doing him an injustice in acknowl-
edging in a man the words of one with whom we spoke when we
prayed to God; we are usually at a loss and try to change the
meaning. . . .

Our thoughts must then be awakened to keep their vigil of faith.
We must realize that the one whom we were contemplating a
short time before in his nature as God took to himself the nature
of a servant; he was made in the likeness of men and found to be
a man like others; he humbled himself by being obedient even to

accepting death; as he hung on the cross he made the psalmist's words his own: *My God, my God, why have you forsaken me?*

We pray to him as God, he prays for us as a servant. In the first case he is the Creator, in the second a creature. Himself unchanged, he took to himself our created nature in order to change it, and made us one man with himself, head and body. We pray then to him, through him, in him, and we speak along with him and he along with us.[9]

Our Head Cries Out and Dies

The following citation from the *Commentary on Psalm 140* sharply focuses on the paschal mystery and the real and ontological meaning of the death of the Messiah. What an antidote to some of the sloppy thinking minimizing the meaning of the death of Christ! When one begins to appreciate the meaning of the passion, one sees the whole of human existence in a different and brighter light.

Lord, I have cried to you, hear me. This is a prayer we can all say. This is not my prayer, but that of the whole Christ. Rather, it is said in the name of His body. When Christ was on earth He prayed in His human nature, and prayed to the Father in the name of His body, and when He prayed drops of blood flowed from His whole body. So it is written in the Gospel: *Jesus prayed with earnest prayer, and sweated blood.* What is this blood streaming from his whole body but the martyrdom of the whole Church?

Let my prayer rise like incense in your sight; let the raising of my hands be an evening sacrifice.

This is generally understood of Christ, the head, as every Christian acknowledges. When day was fading into evening, the Lord laid down His life on the cross, to take it up again; He did not lose His life against His will. Here, too, we are symbolized. What part of Him hung on the cross if not the part He had received from us? How could God the Father ever cast off and abandon His only Son, who is indeed one God with Him? Yet Christ, nailing our weakness to the cross (where, as the Apostle says: *Our old nature was nailed to the cross with Him*), cried out with the very voice of our humanity: *My God, my God, why have You forsaken Me?* The evening sacrifice is then the passion of the Lord, the cross of the Lord, the oblation of the victim that brings salvation, the holocaust acceptable to God.[10]

In this profound passage we get a glimpse of an aspect of Christian teaching that I believe is to some extent theologically underdeveloped. It is something that is strongly and nonverbally experienced by the Christian faithful in times of personal suffering or general calamity like war, namely, that in some mysterious way, to use the words of the modern French spiritual writer Leon Bloy, "Christ remains on His cross until the end of the world."[11] He cries out and suffers still in his members. This mystery of Christ's continuing suffering in his members is obvious if one visits the Carmel in Dachau concentration camp; it confronts you in the chapel in Calvary Hospital in the Bronx, where the Stations of the Cross symbolically show the suffering Christ manifesting the symptoms of advanced cancer.

Of course Augustine in many sermons and writings makes it very clear that Christ died for us collectively as well as individually. One could fill a book with these quotations. But the great bishop never stopped at this contemplation of the love of God for us. He constantly called upon those who believed to respond with love for their fellow members of the Mystical Body and those who were potentially members, those outside the church. In the *Commentary on the Gospel of St. John* (tract 84) he calls upon us to imitate the martyrs who laid down their lives for their brethren in imitation of Christ. He speaks of the liturgical commemoration of the martyrs which implores their prayers, distinguishing this commemoration from that of the other dead for whom we pray. Perhaps he was thinking here of the fervent appeal that his mother made before her death—that her sons pray for her at the altar of God (*Confessions* 9.11). In the following text (which is read at the Office of Readings on Wednesday of Holy Week), the Eucharist and the sacrificial death of Christ, the marvelous witness and prayer for the dead, all come together around the theme of the table of the Lord.

Dear brethren, the Lord has marked out for us the fullness of love that we ought to have for each other. He tells us: *No one has greater love than the man who lays down his life for his friends.* In these words, the Lord tells us what the perfect love we should have for one another involves. John, the evangelist who recorded them, draws the conclusion in one of his letters: *As Christ laid down his life for us, so we too ought to lay down our lives for our brothers.*

This is surely what we read in the Proverbs of Solomon: *If you sit down to eat at the table of a ruler, observe carefully what is set before you; then stretch out your hand, knowing that you must provide the same kind of meal yourself.* What is this ruler's table if not the one at which we receive the body and blood of him who laid down his life for us? What does it mean to sit at this table if not to approach it with humility? What does it mean to observe carefully what is set before you if not to meditate devoutly on so great a gift? What does it mean to stretch out one's hand, knowing that one must provide the same kind of meal oneself, if not what I have just said: as Christ laid down his life for us, so we in our turn ought to lay down our lives for our brothers? This is what the apostle Paul said: *Christ suffered for us, leaving us an example, that we might follow in his footsteps.*

At this table of the Lord we do not commemorate the martyrs in the same way as we commemorate others who rest in peace. We do not pray for the martyrs as we pray for those others, rather, they pray for us, that we may follow in their footsteps. They practiced the perfect love of which the Lord said there could be none greater. They provided "the same kind of meal" as they had themselves received at the Lord's table.[12]

The Church Rejoices at the Risen Lord

The resurrection of Christ is an event that comes to its full meaning only because of its acknowledgment and celebration in the whole church. Without this miracle the church, the city of the Lord of Hosts, would not exist, but it is now spread throughout the earth. It is also obvious that the great struggles the church was having at this time (with the Aryans, Donatists, Pelagians, and the barbarians) had some people fearful that the church was about to be destroyed. Augustine reassures them. This reassurance, which certainly and appropriately needs to be reheard in our disturbed times, is given in the *Sermon on the Psalms* (47) and is read in the Liturgy of the Hours on Wednesday, the nineteenth week of the year.

As we have heard, so also have we seen. Truly blessed Church! You have both heard and seen. Your have heard the promises, and you see their fulfillment; you have heard in prophecy, and you see in the Gospel. Yes, all that has now been brought to completion was prophesied in times past. Raise up your eyes, then, and cast your gaze around the world. See God's people, your heritage, spread to the ends of the earth. See him whose hands and feet were pierced by nails, whose bones were numbered as they hung upon the wood, and for whose garments they cast lots. See Him reigning, whom they saw hanging upon the cross; see Him enthroned in heaven, whom they despised when He walked on the earth. See the word fulfilled: *All the ends of the earth shall turn to the Lord, and all nations shall worship in his sight.* See all this and shout with joy: *As we have heard, so also have we seen.*[13]

The Faithful Ascend with Christ

If Christ still mystically suffers in his wounded members on earth, then they in turn rejoice with him in heaven although still on earth. This belief, so boldly stated by Augustine, is not often preached or even frequently talked about by theologians because, candidly, it seems so contrary to one's everyday experience. It was the same for the embattled old bishop. No one has ever accused the bishop of Hippo of looking at life through rose-colored glasses. He is once supposed to have remarked wryly: "Don't cry for the dead, cry for the living." Drawing on the mysterious and paradoxical words of our Savior, "No one has ever ascended into heaven, except the one who descended from heaven, the Son of Man, who is in heaven." Augustine points out that Christ in some way as Word of God remained united with the Godhead even while he suffered on earth. So as we suffer in union with Christ in the Mystical Body, we are in some mysterious way abiding in heaven. And some people thought Augustine was a pessimist. To join his realism with his mystical optimism here expressed is a *tour de force,* seen clearly in the following reading for the feast of the Ascension.

Today our Lord Jesus Christ ascended into heaven; let our hearts ascend with Him. Listen to the words of the Apostle: *If you have risen with Christ, set your hearts on the things that are above where Christ is, seated at the right hand of God; seek the things that are above, not the things that are on earth.* For just as he remained with us even after his ascension, so we too are already in heaven with him, even though what is promised us has not yet been fulfilled in our bodies.

Christ is now exalted above the heavens, but he still suffers on earth all the pain that we, the members of his body, have to bear. He showed this when He cried out from above: *Saul, Saul, why do you persecute me?* and when He said: *I was hungry and you gave me food.*

Why do we on earth not strive to find rest with Him in heaven even now, through the faith, hope and love that unites us to Him? While in heaven He is also with us; and we while on earth are with Him. He is here with us by His divinity, His power and His love. We cannot be in heaven, as He is on earth, by divinity, but in Him, we can be there by love.[14]

He Will Come!

As we know from reading the New Testament, especially St. Paul and the book of Revelation, Christians in ancient times expected Christ to return to judge the world, whose end would be in the foreseeable future. Obviously they were wrong in some sense, although two thousand years is just a weekend in astronomical time and not even very long if we consider the age of the human race. Augustine in this sermon emphasizes, as do the parables of our Lord, that we ought to be getting ourselves ready. In a number of places he focuses on the observable fact that his hearers will be facing death soon and consequently should be using every day to get ready by living a righteous life.

In the following sermon on Psalm 95 he uses the certainty of the last judgment to encourage people to live by the first coming of Christ (the whole of the New Testament) so they may get ready for the second. Unfortunately, we do not hear this very often because our age has chosen to ignore the reality of judgment and the possibility of eternal loss. As I write these lines I am still emotionally trying to recover from a pilgrimage to the concentration camp at Auschwitz and especially to the bunker where St. Maximillian Kobe was starved to death and to the gas chambers where hundreds of thousands of Jewish people perished, including Blessed Edith Stein. It was a beautiful sunny day, and I wondered how the sun could even shine on such a place. One comes away from such a place with a very firm conviction that there is a last judgment.

He has come the first time, and He will come again. At His first coming, His own voice declared in the gospel: *Hereafter you shall see the Son of Man coming upon the clouds.* What does he mean by *hereafter?* Does He not mean that the Lord will come at a future time when all the nations of the earth will be striking their breasts in grief? Previously He came through His preachers, and He filled the whole world. Let us not resist His first coming, so that we may not dread the second.

What then should the Christian do? He ought to use the world, not become its slave. And what does this mean?... He who is without anxiety waits without fear until his Lord comes. For what sort of love of Christ is it to fear His coming? Brothers, do we not have to blush for shame? We love Him, yet we fear His coming. Are we really certain that we love Him? Or do we love our sins more? Therefore let us hate our sins and love Him who will exact punishment for them. He will come whether we wish it or not. Do not think that because He is not coming just now, He will not come at all. He will come, you know not when; and provided he finds you prepared, your ignorance of the time of His coming will not be held against you. He has come the first time, and He will come again to judge the earth; He will find those rejoicing who believed in His first coming, *for he has come.*

He will judge the world with equity and the peoples in His truth. What are equity and truth? He will gather together with him for the judgment His chosen ones, but the others He will set apart; for He will place some on His right, others on His left. What is more equitable, what more true than that they should not themselves expect mercy from the judge, who themselves were unwilling to show mercy before the judge's coming. Those, however, who were willing to show mercy will be judged with mercy. For it will be said to those placed on His right: *Come, blessed of my Father, take possession of the kingdom which has been prepared for you from the beginning of the world.*[15]

It would not do justice to St. Augustine to end this survey of his sermons on such a terrifying note. He was not afraid to preach about fear of the Lord. Writing about the text in the Gospel of John 8:49–50, "He (the Father) is the judge," he makes an important distinction between servile and chaste fear. We draw our selection of passages from St. Augustine, the preacher of the Word of God, to a close with this very thought-provoking and down-to-earth citation. The translation is from the Oxford edition.

There is a servile fear, and there is a clean (chaste) fear: there is the fear of suffering punishment, there is another fear of losing righteousness. That fear of suffering punishment is slavish. What great thing is it to fear punishment? The vilest slave and the cruelest robber do so. It is no great thing to fear punishment, but great it is to love righteousness. Has he, then, who loves righteousness no fear? Certainly he has, not of incurring of punishment, but of losing righteousness. So, then, some one is found to be a lover of righteousness, who at heart is much more afraid of its loss, who dreads more being stripped of his righteousness, than thou of thy money. This is the fear that is clean—this (the fear) that endureth for ever. It is not this that love makes away with, or casteth out, but rather embraces it, and keeps it with it, and possesses it as a companion. For we come to the Lord that we may see Him face to face. And there it is this pure fear that preserves us; for such a fear as that does not disturb, but reassures.[16]

Chapter Four

Augustine—The Mystic

Any exploration of the Alpine scene will eventually lead you to the high Alps, to a world of white light and incredible height, different from anything you have ever experienced. You may by this time have guessed that I am not a mountain climber but rather someone who is limited to driving up high ridges and to stopping along lookout areas safely fenced in. But once I was invited to take the cable car high up in the snow fields of the Matterhorn on a bright summer day. It was a different world. It is a similar experience when we survey the mysticism of St. Augustine, and this will be true of any of those rare mystics who are called upon to write of these things. We step out into a different world. Of course, our feet are still firmly on the ground although we are impelled to soar above. How I envied the mountain climbers that day on the Matterhorn when they left us standing at the safe place at the top of the cable car! But at least we can gaze upward to the high peaks, the incredible pinnacles, which few if any human souls have ever explored. You cannot thoughtfully go into the high Alps on the earth or into the mystical mountains and not return a different person.

Although there are some doubters, many have called Augustine the "prince of mystics"[1] or the founding father of Western mysticism.[2] The doubts and debates as to whether Augustine is a mystic have usually arisen because of the need of some writers to use a very constricted definition of a largely indefinable reality or the prejudice of others who cannot bear the thought that someone could be a mystic and at the same time lead the life of a very active bishop and pastor. As Dom Butler has pointed out, there are those who think that being an intellectual, or a person with many cares and responsibilities, or a person with other occupations precludes the possibility of true mystical experience. Augustine writes profoundly but sparingly of his own experience. Yet with very little Christian tradition preceding him on this subject, he paid significant attention in his vast writings to the mystical element in the teachings of Scriptures and in the life of the church. As we shall see, his teaching on the mystical side of Christian experience has guided many, if not most, solid writers who came after him up until this very day.

What Does "Mystical" Mean?

A word should be said about the term "mystical." Like love, this word has many meanings. It has its origins in the Greek verb meaning "to close one's eyes" and the first definition of the word is "invisible" or "secret." This term "mystical" was used by St. Augustine and other fathers to describe (1) the hidden and deeper meanings of the bible; (2) spiritual realities that are intangible, like the effects of Christ's passion in our lives or the sacramental signs like the Eucharist; (3) miracles; and (4) the church itself, which is the Mystical Body of Christ. Doctor McGinn, who includes a very helpful analysis of this term and its application to Augustine's life and works, writes: "This sense of Christianity as containing an inner dimension in which the believer is called to participate through incorporation into Christ at baptism is the implicit ground of Augustine's 'mysticism.' . . . [H]is sense of the necessity for all Christians to penetrate into the depths of this mystery in order to find, to touch, and even to see God created the theological foundation upon which more explicit mystical theories were later constructed in Latin Christianity."[3]

There are a number of fascinating and profound questions related to Augustine's spiritual teachings and the precise meaning of the word "mystic" when applied to him (and, I might add, to several of the fathers of the church) that go beyond the scope of this book for beginners in Augustinian studies. To lead beginners up into greater heights and to alleviate my own frustration at not being able even to present these questions, I suggest the following readings in this order. Sister Clark's excellent introduction and selected readings in *Augustine of Hippo*. You should run and not walk to the nearest bookshop and obtain this volume of the Classics of Western Spirituality series.[4] Then you should find a good Catholic library where Dom Cuthbert Butler's *Western Mysticism* can be found. It has appeared in several editions over the years and is now available in paperback. This study is, in fact, fairly easy to read and does not assume a great deal of background although it helps to know a little Latin. Then you should be prepared to work on Dr. Bernard McGinn's *Foundations of Mysticism*, which is in every sense of the word a work of great scholarship. I believe he has broken new ground in Augustinian studies with his original analysis of the steps to contemplation in Augustine. It would be well to read the whole book and not to start with chapter 7 on Augustine, but if you like to cheat a little you can start there and then you will certainly go back and read the whole book. From these sources you will be led to a number of profound studies by great scholars who generally do not write in a popular vein but whom you should then be prepared to read.

Augustine's Experience of God

We will follow the simplest outline possible of Augustine's insights on the Christian's road to the partial knowledge and vision of God in this life, preparing us for the blessedness of that total experience in the life to come. The essential steps in this process may already be familiar, but we will see that Augustine adds insights especially on the image of God and the Trinity which are his own. Following the lead of Dom Butler, we adopt Augustine's splendid commentary on Psalm 41 as our outline. Commenting on this remarkable document Dom Butler writes: "However little it may express of the real thoughts of the Psalmist, still, without doing violence to the text, it makes his words with rare skill serve as a statement of mystical doctrine forestalling the lines laid down by the great mystics of later times."[5] (Since Dom Butler was using the Oxford scholars'

"Library of the Fathers" we shall use this translation despite its somewhat stilted Victorian prose.)

Like as the hart desireth the water-brooks, so longeth my soul after Thee, O God.

This psalm is sung as 'a Psalm for Understanding' (title). For what understanding is it sung? Come, my brethren, catch my eagerness; share with me in this my longing: let us both love, let us both be influenced with this thirst, let us both hasten to the well of understanding. Let us then long for it as the hart for the brook; let us long for that fountain whereof another Scripture saith, *For with Thee is the fountain of life.*

The Desire for Truth, Light and Beauty—All in God

As much as Augustine is a disciple of the truth, and following both Scripture (especially Christ in the Gospel of John) and the Neoplatonic philosophers, he begins with desire. In the *Confessions* we have already seen that the desire for God as the source of beauty and truth is the beginning of Augustine's spiritual journey. "Come Lord, work upon us, call us back, set us on fire and clasp us close, be fragrant to us, draw us to thy loveliness; let us love, let us run to Thee" (8.4). "You have pierced our hearts with the arrow of Your love, and our minds were pierced with the arrows of your words" (9.2).

The following passage is used by Augustine in the time between his experience of conversion (8.12) and his baptism by St. Ambrose. Like so many psalms, it brings out his burning desire for God. He had been meditating on Psalm 4.

It was with a deep cry of my heart that I uttered the next verse: *O in peace! O in selfsame!* O how he has said: *I will sleep and I will rest.* For who shall stand against us *when the saying that is written will come to pass: Death is swallowed up in victory?* You supremely are that selfsame, for you are not changed and in You is that rest in which all cares are forgotten, since there is no other besides You, and we have not to seek other things which are not what You are: but You, Lord, alone have *made me dwell in hope.*

All these things I read and was on fire; nor could I find what could be done with those deaf dead, of whom indeed I had myself been one for I had been a scourge, a blind raging snarler against the Scriptures, which are all honeyed with the honey of heaven and all luminous with Your light: and now I was fretting my heart out over the enemies of these same Scriptures. (*Conf.* 9.4)

This text also focuses on the desire of Augustine for the light of truth. One will never understand this great bishop unless one meditates for a time on the fact that Augustine had a passionate desire, almost a sensual desire, like one might have for beauty or even food or air, but in this case it was for the truth. It is this powerful inclination motivated by grace that makes the first step toward the spiritual life even possible. One will never be able to enter into the Augustinian experience if one has not felt some of this thirst, although one may have a profound historical or intellectual appreciation of him. And not everyone who experiences this thirst will arrive at the fountain of contemplation because there are many possible detours along the way and the thirst itself may become a distant memory, in fact a haunting ghost which embitters the person later on. Bertrand Russell, who early in his life wrote positively of the thirst for God and then became a bitter atheist and a hater of all religion, might be an example of such a disaster.

Another aspect of Augustine's spirituality becomes obvious— the linking of beauty and truth with the desire for that which fills the longing of both the heart and the mind. Truth is certainly represented by the analogy of light, but many years of reading Augustine have convinced me that he did not mean by truth what was logically correct or even intellectually valid but the experience of what reality in fact is, as it is perceived by intellect and intuition. This is a higher form of knowledge that goes beyond discursive reasoning.

For He is both the Fountain and the Light; for it is *in Thy Light that we shall see light.* If He is both the Fountain and the Light, with good reason is He the Understanding also, because He both filleth the soul that thirsteth for knowledge, and every one who hath "understanding" is enlightened by a certain light; not a corporeal, not a carnal one, not an outward, but an inward light! There is, then, a certain light within, not possessed by those who understand not. Run to the brooks; long after the water-brooks, *With God is the fountain of Life;* a fountain that shall never be dried up: in His light is a light that shall never be darkened. Long thou for this light: for a certain fountain, a certain light, such as Thy bodily eyes know not; a light, to see which the inward eye must be prepared; a fountain, to drink of which the inward thirst is to be kindled. Run to the fountain; long for the fountain; but do it not anyhow, be not satisfied with running like any ordinary animal; run thou like the hart.[6]

The Destruction of Vices

The next great passage is based on the notion that the hart or wild deer killed serpents and then was very thirsty afterwards. This analogy illustrates much that is critical for the spiritual quest according to any classical author—our vices must be purged. This is the first step of the spiritual journey, and the earnest aspirant is warned not to compromise. Augustine, in the *Confessions,* describes how he attacked his own deep seated vices with fervor. He has more importantly, however, left us psychologically insightful accounts of the long battles he had to fight with himself against himself.

But perhaps Scripture meant us to consider in the hart another point also. The hart destroys serpents, and after the killing of serpents, it is inflamed with thirst yet more violent. The serpents are thy vices; destroy the serpents of iniquity, then wilt thou long yet more for the Fountain of Truth. Whilst thou are yet indulgent to thy vices, thy covetousness or thy appetite, when am I to find in thee a longing such as this, that might make thee run to the water-brooks? When are thou to desire the Fountain of Wisdom, whilst thou are yet labouring in the venom of iniquity? Destroy in thyself whatever is contrary to the truth, and when thou hast seen thyself to be comparatively free from irrational passions, be not contented to stay where thou art, as if there was nothing further for thee to long for. For there is yet somewhat to which thou mayest raise thyself, even if thou hast already achieved that triumph within, that there is no longer within thee a foe to hinder and to thwart thee. For perhaps if thou are the hart, thou wilt already say to me: "God knows that I am no longer covetous, that I no longer set my heart on the property of any man; that I am not inflamed by the passion of unlawful love; that I do not pine away with hatred or ill-will against any man"; and as to all other things of this description, thou wilt say: "I am free from them"; and perhaps thou wouldest fain know wherein thou mayest find pleasure. Long for the water-brooks; God hath wherewith to refresh thee, and to satisfy thee when thou comest to Him, athirst, like the swift-footed hart, after the destruction of the serpents.[7]

Dom Butler reminds us now that "herein lies the feature which marks off true mysticism from the counterfeits which so often, especially in these our days, masquerade in its name. It is the constant teaching of the great mystics that there can be no progress in prayer without mortification; no contemplation without self denial and self discipline seriously undertaken; no real mysticism without asceticism; in its full sense of spiritual training. After all, this is only the teaching of the Gospel: the clean of heart shall see God."[8] It is worth noting at this silly time, the end of the twentieth century, that the struggle with vices is almost ignored even by genuinely religious people. Often the sincerely devout of our time seem to have little or no qualms of conscience about uncharitableness, detraction, calumny, and impatience especially if these vices have become part of the functioning of their personality and have become linked with the habitual way they pursue their religious goals. However good these goals may be in themselves, one is struck by the lack of self-knowledge and discipline even on the part of those who are devout. It is fairly obvious that some well-intentional spiritual writers display little working concept of fidelity or loyalty to legitimate authority, which is really far more important than the selective observance of this or that letter of the law. This is a time of few harts and lots of snakes, so be careful.

Such a hart then, being yet in a state of "faith" only, not yet in "sight" of what he believes, has to bear with adversaries, who mock the man who believes, and cannot show them that in which he believes, saying, *Where is thy God?* Meditating night and day on this taunt, I have myself sought to find my God, that if I could I might not believe only, but might see also somewhat. For I see the things which my God hath made, but my God Himself I do not see.[9]

The Search for God in His Creation

Butler comments: The effort of mind to attain to the knowledge and sight of God through creatures is described in a striking passage: Augustine interrogates the earth, the heavenly bodies, his own body, his soul in its highest and most spiritual mental operations. He goes on:

> Is God, then, anything of the same nature as the soul? This mind of ours seeks to find something that is God. It seeks to find a Truth not subject to change, a Substance not capable of failing. The mind itself is not of this nature: it is capable of progress and of decay, of knowledge and of ignorance, of remembering or forgetting. That mutability is not incident to God.[10]

The struggle in the spiritual life is a long one, and the individual is operating on faith and not on vision or powerful experiences of God's presence. Our adversaries come from without but especially from within—our own doubts, needs, and passions. Many for years repeat the question "Where is your God?" Despite the conflict herein described, Dom Butler sees in the following text what he calls the fundamental postulate of mysticism—at least according to St. Augustine—that it is possible in this life to "see somewhat of God, to have an experiential perception of Him."[11]

Augustine seeks God in external creation and then in his own soul. He goes on:

Having therefore sought to find my God in visible and corporeal things, and found Him not; having sought to find His Substance in myself, and found Him not, I perceive my God to be something higher than my soul. Therefore that I might attain unto Him *I thought on these things, and poured out my soul above myself.* When would my soul attain to that object of its search, which is "above my soul," if my soul were not to pour itself out above itself? For were it to rest in itself, it would not see anything else beyond itself; and in seeing itself, would not, for all that, see God. . . . I, so long as I do not *see,* so long as my happiness is postponed, *Make my tears my bread day and night.* I seek my God in every corporeal nature, terrestrial or celestial, and find Him not: I seek His Substance in my own soul, and I find it not; yet still have I thought on these things, and wishing to see *the invisible things of my God, being understood by the things made,* I have poured forth my soul above myself, and there remains no longer any being for me to attain to save my God. For it is *there* is the "house of my God." His dwelling-place is above my soul; from thence He beholds me; from thence He governs me and provides for me; from thence He appeals to me, and calls me, and directs me; leads me in the way, and to the end of my way.[12]

It would seem to me that here Augustine describes what would come to be called the illuminative way. The format of the psalm unfortunately does not give him an opportunity here to examine the various steps in detail, but they are to be found in his writings and, in fact, they are found a little later in this commentary. The individual reader may find it helpful to review some of these steps in my book *Spiritual Passages,* where they are presented with a distinct Augustinian flavor.[13]

Finding God in the Church

We now come to a very powerful Augustinian theme: The highest contemplative prayer is to be found in the things of the church and not in the solitary experience of the soul. Here Augustine goes beyond the influence of the non-Christian philosopher Plotinus. This important Platonist had given him much of the foundation of his earlier thinking about coming to the knowledge of God. He is now clearly left behind. Augustine deeply holds not only that God must call and lead us to his grace but that we must find him in the church, of which the head is Christ, the great and single mediator between God and the human race. Doctor McGinn comments: "The ascent is possible only through the

agency of the Church; indeed, Augustine argues that it is by meditating on the virtues of the saints, the *membra tabernaculi,* that
ecstatic transition comes about, an unusual idea as Butler noted,
but one fully in harmony with the indispensably ecclesial nature
of Augustine's mystical thought."[14]

Augustine in his commentary now makes very clear the essential role of the community of believers, the church.

But He Who has His house very high in secret place, hath also on
earth a tabernacle. His tabernacle on earth is the Church. It is
here that He is to be sought, for it is in the tabernacle that is found
the way by which we arrive at the house. *For I will go into the
place of Thy admirable tabernacle, even unto the house of God.*
God's tabernacle on earth is the Faithful. How much is there I
admire in this tabernacle: —the self-conquest and the virtues of
God's servants. I admire the presence of those virtues in the soul;
but still I am walking in *the place of the tabernacle.* I pass beyond
these also; and admirable though the tabernacle be, yet when I
come to *the house of God,* I am even struck dumb with astonish-
ment. It is there, in the sanctuary of God, in the house of God, is
the fountain of understanding. It was going up to the tabernacle
the Psalmist arrived at the house of God. It was thus, that whilst
admiring the members of the tabernacle, he was led on to the
house of God: by following the leadings of a certain delight, an
inward mysterious and hidden pleasure, as if from the house of
God there sounded sweetly some instrument; and he, whilst
walking in the tabernacle, hearing a certain inward sound, led on
by its sweetness, and following the guidance of the sound, with-
drawing himself from all noise of flesh and blood, made his way
on even to the house of God. In the house of God there is a
never-ending festival; the angelic choir makes an eternal holiday,
the presence of God's face, joy that never fails. From that everlasting, perpetual festivity there sounds in the ears of the heart a
mysterious strain, melodious and sweet, provided only the world
does not drown the sounds. As he walks in this tabernacle, and
considers God's wonderful works for the redemption of the faithful, the sound of that festivity charms his ears and bears the *hart*
away to the *water-brooks.*[15]

This description of the experience of God in the church, linking the life of the faithful Christian with the life of the saints in heaven, is a key teaching of the fathers and is, in fact, most powerfully symbolized in the celebration of the divine liturgy in the Eastern Church. However, the link between the prayer of the church on earth and the worship of the church in heaven, led by its divine founder and head, was strongly restated in modern times in the magnificent but almost forgotten encyclical of Pope Pius XII, *Mediator Dei*. Because the liturgy is so often poorly celebrated or when it is done well there is so frequently much more attention paid to accidents than to essentials, it may seem far-fetched to the serious reader at the end of the twentieth century to see the contemplative experience linked with the mysteries of the church. The next passage in Augustine's commentary on the psalm may shed some light on this problem, which reflects the struggle with the doldrums of mediocrity. As I read it over I could only think of the saying of Scott Hahn, one of the Protestant clergy who recently entered into full communion with the Catholic Church: "Come on in, it's awful." The contrast is between the tabernacle or the pilgrim church and the house of God in heaven. What Augustine is doing here is returning to the struggles of the believers trying to come closer to God. The structure of the psalm in verse 7 did not permit him, apparently, to grant these struggles as full a treatment as he might have wished.

But seeing that "the corruptible body presseth down the soul," even though we have in some way dispersed the clouds by walking as longing leads us on, and for a brief while have come within reach of that sound, so that by an effort we may catch something from that house of God; yet through the burden, so to speak, of our infirmity, we sink back to our usual level and relapse to our ordinary state (*consueta*). And just as there we found cause for rejoicing, so here there will not be wanting an occasion for sorrow. For that hart that *made tears its bread day and night*, borne along by *longing to the water-brooks* (that is, to the inward sweetness of God), *pouring forth his soul above himself*, that he may attain to what is above his own soul, walking *unto the place of the admirable tabernacle, even unto the house of God*, and led on by the delight of that inward spiritual sound to feel contempt for exterior things and be ravished by things interior, is but a mortal man still; is still groaning here, still bearing about the frailty of the flesh, still in peril in the midst of the offences of this world. He therefore gazes on himself, as if he were coming from that other world; and says to himself, now placed in the midst of these sorrows, comparing these with the things to see which he had entered in there, and after seeing which he had come forth from thence, *"Why art thou cast down, O my soul, and why dost thou disquiet me?"*[16]

When we introduced the readers to book 10 of the *Confessions* we included several passages in which Augustine deeply laments the struggles of this life which interfere with the contemplation of God (see chapter 1). It would seem to be common enough in mystical literature to hear about the special pain and sorrow of having at times been in touch with the vision of God or at least the profound experience of his presence and then to have to return to the everyday business of struggling with the concerns of life and the battle with our own vices. This theme runs through many medieval mystics and is most strongly expressed by Blessed Henry Suso.[17]

The way to God is long and weary for two reason. One is inherent in the nature of things, the contrast between the limitations of the human mind and soul and the transcendent object of our desires. This is true since the fall of the human race and the loss of our innocence.[18] It is also true because of the cupidity of the individual. In fact, some individuals seek after God with much more determination and purity of heart than others. But even these struggle along as we see in the lives of the saints. The first difficulty, that is, human limitation, is highlighted in the following text:

What else therefore do we do when we study to be wise, except to concentrate our whole soul with all the ardor we can upon what we touch with our mind, and as it were place it there and fix it unshakably; so that it may no longer enjoy privately what has entangled it in passing things, but freed from all influence of times or places may lay hold on that which is ever one and the same. For just as the soul is the whole life of the body, the happy life of the soul is God. While we do this, and until we have completed it, we are on the way. And it is granted to us to rejoice in these true and sure goods, albeit they are as yet but flickering lights on this dark road. (*On Free Choice* 2.16)[19]

A far greater and more persistent sorrow comes from the second difficulty of the human being, that is, the inconsistency of the will and confusion of the mind in seeking after God. Augustine would often speak of this throughout his life, but no passage is more expressive than this well-known one from the *Confessions.*

When once I shall be united to Thee with all my being, there shall be no more grief and toil, and my life will be alive, filled wholly with Thee. Thou dost raise up him whom Thou dost fill; whereas being not yet filled with Thee I am a burden to myself. The pleasures of this life for which I should weep are in conflict with the sorrows of this life in which I should rejoice, and I know not on which side stands the victory. Woe is me, Lord, have pity on me! For I have likewise sorrows which are evil and these are in conflict with joys that are good, and I know not on which side stands the victory. See, I do not hide my wounds: Thou are the physician, I the sick man; Thou are merciful, I need mercy. (*Conf.* 10.28, 29)

The Vision of God in This Life

We have reviewed briefly with the help of the commentary on Psalm 41 Augustine's teaching on the first two stages of the spiritual journey. What about his teaching on union with God, the so called unitive way? Great debates have gone on for centuries over what Augustine (or any other great mystic for that matter) meant by saying that they had a vision of God or even the meaning of the less disconcerting phrase, the experience of God. Often in such debates I think of G. K. Chesterton's warning about not trying to "ef" the ineffable. We have already seen that for Augustine the full experience of God and the happiness it brings await eternity and are completely a grace merited by Christ, not something that humans can accomplish—contrary to what some of these old Platonist teachers may have thought. We have also seen that Augustine locates the possibility of the partial vision of God in the life of the Church and even suggests that the contemplation of the virtues of the saints may be a road to a certain vision of God. (This devout suggestion certainly will not meet much enthusiasm in certain corners at the moment.)

Doctor McGinn gives a remarkably well-informed and carefully thought-out presentation on the Augustinian vision of God which is a delight to study but only when one is prepared. Here we will present a few quotations to get the reader thinking about this question: What does one see or know in this life when one experiences the presence of God at a deeper level than the simple intellectual conviction bolstered by faith and Scripture and theological teaching that "in him we live and move and have our being."

Writing of the most significant times in his life, the months before his conversion, St. Augustine pointedly mentions that he had been reading his old Platonist teachers. This suggests, according to Dr. McGinn, that he intended to use some of their formulations in his description of religious experience. One cannot fail to speculate a millennium and a half later if Augustine used these formulations as a sort of an *apologia* to assist in the conversion of the Platonists or because they were the ways that he experienced and thought about life himself. I prefer the latter answer because these passages seem to represent Augustine's experience with such spontaneity and authenticity that I find it distasteful to think that these words were fashioned for pragmatic reasons, however well intended. I have personally related to Augustine's description of the experience of God with such a total and unqualified involvement for so many years beginning in adolescence that it never dawned on me to even ask why he had written as he did. These phrases always seemed obvious to me as they do now: "the eye of my soul," "the weakness of my gaze," "shaken with love and dread," and even "the unchangeable light." When I read these words in high school I scarcely knew who Plato was, and I had never heard of Plotinus. I suspect there are many other people who are no more mystics than I am but who, reading these blazing words of the *Confessions* and even the later works, know what Augustine means because these words express their own search for the God of light and beauty. Please read the following passage and see if it speaks to you:

Being admonished by all this to return to myself, I entered into my own depths, with You as guide; and I was able to do it because You were my helper. I entered, and with the eye of my soul, such as it was, I saw Your unchangeable Light shining over that same eye of my soul, over my mind. It was not the light of every day that the eye of flesh can see, nor some greater light of the same order, such as might be if the brightness of our daily light should be seen shining with a more intense brightness and filling all things with its greatness. Your Light was not that, but other, altogether other, than all such lights. Nor was it above my mind as oil above the water it floats on, nor as the sky is above the earth; it was above because it made me, and I was below because made by it. He who knows the truth knows that Light, and he that knows the Light knows eternity. Charity knows it. O eternal truth and true love and beloved eternity! Thou art my God , I sigh to Thee by day and by night. When first I knew Thee, Thou didst lift me up so that I might see that there was something to see, but that I was not yet the man to see it. And Thou didst beat back the weakness of my gaze, blazing upon me too strongly, and I was shaken with love and with dread. And I knew that I was far from Thee in the region of unlikeness, as if I heard Thy voice from on high: "I am the food of grown men: grow and you shall eat Me. And You shall not change Me into yourself as bodily food, but into Me you shall be changed." And I learned that *Thou hast corrected man for iniquity and Thou didst make my soul shrivel up like a moth.* And I said "Is truth then nothing at all, since it is not extended either through finite spaces or infinite?" And Thou didst cry to me from afar: "I am who am." And I heard Thee, as one hears in the heart; and there was from that moment no ground of doubt in me: I would more easily have doubted my own life than have doubted that truth is: which is *clearly seen, being understood by the things that are made. (Conf.* 7.10, 11)

The quotation that tells us so much about Augustine's experience is, of course, the one we have already given in our brief review of the *Confessions* in chapter 1, the so-called episode at the window in Ostia (11.10). The reader should go back now and re-read these pages (see pp. 31–32 above), paying close attention to the following:

(1) Augustine brings you through the process of "touching and hearing God" twice in the text.

(2) Both times he stresses the idea that one must go beyond a sense of perception and even beyond the lessons of Scripture

that—"the darkness of parable"—not because of their lack of divine authority but because they are pointers to the great reality beyond: finding God even beyond the soul itself. These are ideas of ascent borrowed partially from the Platonists and partly from the Scriptures.

(3) The key words are mysterious, that is, expressions of mystical reality "raising ourselves to the self-same" (*idipsum*, that is, God who is complete in himself); also "with all the effort of our heart we did for one instant attain to touch it" and "we should hear Himself in whom all these things we love." Doctor McGinn's translation is, I think, even more accurate than Mr. Sheed's, which we have been using. He translates *toto ictu cordis* as "with the whole beat of the heart."[20]

It is important to note something we have seen before, that the analogies used are both of the mind (to hear and to know) and of the heart. As Dr. McGinn points out, referring to this text, we observe the consistent Augustinian linkage of knowledge and love. Love and knowledge are intertwined in Augustine's mystical consciousness.[21] This linking of love and knowledge will have profound influence down through the centuries, and, although it is by no means a formulation unique to Augustine, his supremacy as the theologian of the Western church for almost eight hundred years to the time of St. Thomas Aquinas explains its wide acceptance.

As a Capuchin seminarian in the twentieth century, I prayed with my fellow students before class a prayer that linked knowledge with love: "I do not wish to know you except that I may love you." St. Bonaventure would say the same thing.

> In this passing over, if it is to be perfect, all intellectual activities must be left behind and the height of our affection must be totally transferred and transformed into God.[22]

These words all seem to disparage knowledge, but they link love with knowledge, giving love the first place. The fact that they link the two speaks of Augustine's influence on later ages and is in contrast with the decidedly gnostic view popular with the Platonists of long ago and even with some of the ersatz gnosticism of the present time.

Do We See a Divine Essence?

No one thinks that Augustine in his many descriptions of seeing, knowing, and loving God was implying that the heavenly grace of knowing God as he is in his essence is the highest accomplishment of the spiritual life in this world. The following quotation from the *Confessions* is completely consistent with Augustine's life-long conviction that we have only a partial and passing experience of God:

Where have You not walked with me, O Truth, teaching me both what to shun and what to seek, when I set before You such things as I have been able to see here below and begged Your counsel? With my bodily senses I surveyed the external world as best I could, and considered the life my body has from me and the senses themselves. From that I turned inward to the depths of my memory, like so many vast rooms filled so wonderfully with things beyond number: and I considered and stood awe-stricken: for no one of these could I discern without You, and I found that no one of these was You. Nor was I their finder. . . . Nor in all these things that my mind traverses in search of You, do I find any sure place for my mind save in You, in whom all that is scattered in me is brought into one, so that nothing of me may depart from You. And sometimes You admit me to a state of mind that I am not ordinarily in, a kind of delight which could it ever be made permanent in me would be hard to distinguish from the life to come. But by the weight of my imperfections I fall back again, and I am swallowed up by things customary: I am bound, and I weep bitterly, but I am bitterly bound. So much does the burden of custom count for. I can remain in my ordinary state though unwilling, I would remain in that other state but am not able, in both states I know my misery. (*Conf.* 10.40)

He goes on to the question again fifteen years later (in 413) in his well-known letter to Pauline, *Letter* 147. An excellent translation of this letter by Sr. Clark is found in *Augustine of Hippo*. There is no question that the seeing of God "face to face" (Genesis 32:20) is the experience of the saints in heaven. Augustine discusses the very special cases of Moses, St. Paul, and St. John. This discussion along with further debates on whether he changed his mind from his original view that Moses did see God as the saints do in heaven is beyond the scope of an introduction. Dom Butler and Dr. McGinn both discuss this subject.

What is far more important for the spiritual life of the individual reader is that for most sincere seekers of God this experience of him is partial and fleeting in this life. With much insight, Sr. Clark sees Augustine's opinion, especially in the *Letter on the Vision of God,* as an expression of his negative theology and of his great reliance on faith.[23] The reader may not be familiar with the term "negative theology," which means, to put it simply, that we come to appreciate God's transcendence by the recognition of what we do not know or the experience of what we lack in our efforts to see God. The term "apophatic" from the Greek word meaning "to be without light" is properly used to describe this kind of teaching. On an affective level, it is often observed that "absence makes the heart grow fonder" or "distance lends enchantment." These terms can be analogues of the apophatic experience of God which St. John of the Cross summed up in his famous "Nada" or "Nothing." Although there are many examples of the beginning of an apophatic theology in St. Augustine (and some of the other fathers, especially his contemporary St. Gregory of Nyssa, whose books he did not see), the Christian world would wait for a more developed statement of the *via negativa* until the sixth-century writer known as the Pseudo-Dionysius (or simply Dionysius). This anonymous Syrian monk would take up from the fathers before him and write powerfully on knowing and loving God by dark knowledge, echoing the psalm "Truly Thou are a hidden God." Saint John of the Cross would be the great link of this kind of knowledge with modern times. One must also mention the English mystics and especially the author of the *Cloud of Unknowing.* For the reader unfamiliar with this concept it is expressed so well in the old translation of St. Paul's words: "We see now through a glass darkly" (1 Corinthians 13:12).

The Goal of the Spiritual Life

If the goal of the spiritual journey is only a partial and fleeting vision of God in this world, then what, according to Augustine, is the highest peak of spiritual development possible? A certain union with God in this life is spoken of by the Neoplatonists, and a very real union is the constant theme of the later Christian mystical writers. In fact, the goal is called the unitive way. Even Augustine's later disciples, like St. Bernard and St. Bonaventure, would speak of such a union, and some would even use metaphors drawn from human love, especially in the Song of Songs, as did St. John of the Cross. Saint Augustine simply does not speak in this way. However, the idea of union is not at all foreign to him, but his idea of union is our union with Christ as members of his body. Doctor McGinn suggests that Augustine's deliberate avoidance of the language of union was an implied criticism of the limitations of non-Christian mystical efforts like those of Plotinus. He states: "Union is important for Augustine, but only as our union with the Word made flesh—precisely the point where the pagan Platonists went wrong! This loving union we enjoy with all the brethren in the community of the church makes possible the brief experiences of the vision of God that can sometimes be enjoyed in this life."[24]

A Half Original Idea

With great trepidation, as an Augustinian amateur, I would like to make a distinction which, in keeping with my stated purpose, is not very original. When the question is asked in this way: (1) Does Augustine speak of an experience of God (*visio Dei*) that is in fact the same thing as the later mystics but using an analogy different from union that is often based on human love and even in some cases sexual union (within the context of deep affection)? (2) If so, then is the union he speaks of with Christ and in and through the church (the union of charity) a means to an end which is personal union with God? or (3) Are the two unions— that with God and that with the church—homologous, that is, similar tendencies going in the same direction like the parallel wheels on the same vehicle. I am not asking these questions to be cute but rather because I have never seen a substantial difference between Augustine's "vision of God" and the "union" of the later mystics.

(1) *Is* Visio Dei *the Same as Union with God?* All the major writers discussing either the transient and profound experiences of God occasionally afforded on the way or the quasi permanent state of mystics in the unitive way are using analogies. This is true if they use the word "vision," an optical analogy lending itself best to an intellectual experience ("I can see it now," we say when comprehending a complex idea). The idea of union with God is also an analogy, but it is obviously not a physical union or even an emotional one the same way that human friendship is. Perhaps the disciples had an emotional friendship with Jesus of Nazareth, but his presence now (for example in eucharistic devotion) is different in many ways. Augustine, while using "vision" but not the word "union," expresses the same idea, according to Dom Butler.[25] Speaking of the experience of God at Ostia (*Confessions* 9.10) Augustine uses these analogies: with burning affection, as our love flamed upward, panting, we touched it with the whole beat of our heart, and sighing. Having become a friar very young, I have never been in love or even had a girlfriend, but it would seem to me that these are hardly intellectual metaphors although in the very same text Augustine uses words more in keeping with "vision" than union: he calls the reality encountered "Wisdom" and "Your Word" and describes the whole experience as "Vision." He concludes this passage with a fascinating point and counterpoint of physical and intellectual analogies when speaking of the life of the saints in eternity: "If all other visions so different be taken away, and this one should so ravish and absorb and wrap the believer in inward joys" (*Confessions* 9.10).

As Dr. McGinn points out, when ten years later in life Augustine wrote the the section on memory in the *Confessions,* he states that this faculty leads one "in the desire to touch you where you can be touched, to cleave to you when such cleaving is possible" (10.17). We have already seen how in the *Homily on Psalm 41* Augustine uses the burning thirst of the hart as an analogue of the desire for God. He uses here the analogy of sweet music coming from the house of God: "It was thus, that whilst admiring the members of your tabernacle (the church) he was led into the house of God: by following the leading of a certain delight and inward and mysterious pleasure as if from the house of God there sounded sweetly some instrument. . . . From that everlasting, perpetual festivity there sounds in the ears of the heart a mysterious strain, melodious and sweet, provided the world does not drown out the sounds."[26]

Music is very often used as an example of loving union—for both heavenly and earthly love. Here the sweet melodies come from the tabernacle, the church, in what seems to be a beautiful harmonizing of the loving union of the soul with God and the sharing of this union with other members of the church.

Both Dom Butler and Dr. McGinn give extensive reviews of Augustine's description and contemplation in this life. These reviews are profound and fascinating but bring us beyond the limit of this book. To draw this question to a close may I simply refer to Augustine's use of the word *amare*, "love." He uses this word of friendship even of nonspiritual friendship in deeply emotional passages on a young friend who died (*Conf.* 4.4–7), of sexual love (*Conf.* 3.1), of true friendship in the Lord (*Conf.* 9.3) referring to his late friend Nebridius, of filial love for his mother (*Conf.* 9.12), and finally of divine love. It would require a whole book to list the times in Augustine that he speaks of the love of God. This same verb, *amare*, "to love," is used throughout. "Late have I loved Thee." It seems obvious to me that this verb with all the uses that Augustine gives it leads to union of mind and heart. When I read the words "Late have I loved Thee" as a youngster and when I read them now they do not mean anything else but what St. Francis, St. Bonaventure, the two Catherines, St. Teresa, St. John of the Cross, and St. Therese of Lisieux meant by the word "love." Nor did any of the true mystics ever suggest that a person in the highest level of the spiritual journey (where they were without admitting it) would remain in a state of mystical union and rapture all the time. In fact, their writings suggest that their experience of union with God was punctuated by distraction, trials, falls, and failures, and even by times of profound darkness and feelings of alienation from God. None of them ever indicated that an awareness of loving union was a constant experience of life. Far from it.

(2) *Is Union with the Members of Christ's Mystical Body a Means to Personal Union with God?* The point made by Dr. McGinn that Augustine also finds union with Christ through the church is obvious to anyone familiar with the bishop and his writings. He is, after St. Paul, the great teacher of the Mystical Body of Christ. And although Augustine's theology is centered on the Trinity rather than on Christ (in this sense not Christocentric) the love of Christ is found everywhere, as we will see presently in the chapter on Augustine as a preacher. The practical aspect of one's love of Christ in the members of his body is fraternal charity, or human kindness and compassion shown to the members of this body. This is the great chain that binds all together in the *vinculum caritatis* of St. Augustine.

In *Sermon* 137, Augustine sums up in a few lines a theme that runs through his later works, namely, that we must love and serve Christ in his members. The whole sermon includes a meditation for the bishop on his responsibilities, a rather severe warning to the clergy (he even speaks of "bad priests"), and an exhortation to the faithful to respond to the zealous example of good clergy.

You are not ignorant believers, my dear friends, and so I know that because your Master in heaven, in whom you have put your hope, has taught you, you have learnt that our Lord Jesus Christ, who has already suffered for us and risen again, is the head of the Church, and the Church is His body, and its health, as it were, exists in the unity of the members in His body and the bond of love which unites them.

Anyone whose love has become cold is sick in the body of Christ. But he, who has already exalted our head, has also the power to heal our sick members as long as they are not cut off by excessive wickedness and cling to the body until they are healed. Any member which still clings to the body has the hope of recovery, but one which has been cut off can neither be healed nor restored. Since then, He is the head of the Church and the Church is His body, the whole Christ is both head and body. He has already risen from the dead. Therefore, our head is in heaven. Our head intercedes for us. Our head, who is sinless and immortal, now propitiates God for our sins, so that we too at last rising again and transfigured in heavenly glory, may follow our head, for where the head is, there too are the rest of the members. But while we are here on earth, we are his members; we must not despair, for we are to follow our head.

Consider, my friends, the love of our head Himself. Although He is already in Heaven, He still suffers on earth as long as the Church suffers here. Here Christ is hungry, thirsty, poor, lonely, sick, and imprisoned. He has told us that He suffers whatever His own body suffers here on earth; on the last day, when He separates His own body and places it on the right, and places the rest, all those who despise Him, on the left, He will say to those on the right: *Come, you whom my Father has blessed, receive the kingdom which has been ready for you since the beginning of the world* (Matthew 25:34).

What have they done to deserve this? *For I was hungry, and you gave me food* (Matthew 25:35); and so His narration continues, as if it were He Himself who had received their kindly attentions, till at last they ask in bewilderment, *Lord, when did we see you hungry, a stranger, and in prison?* (Matthew 25:39) And He tells them: *Whatever you did for the least of my people you did for me* (Matthew 25:40). Thus, even in our own bodies, our heads are above and our feet on the ground. Yet when someone treads on your foot in a crowd, is it not your head which says, You are treading on me? No one has trodden on your head, nor on your tongue. Your head is above, in safety; nothing has harmed it. Yet, because of the bond of love which unites our bodies from head to foot, the tongue did not keep aloof from the foot, but said, You are treading on me, although no one had touched it.

Thus, as the tongue, which no one has touched, says, You are treading on me, so Christ the head, whom no one treads on, says, *I was hungry, and you gave me food.* And to those who failed to do this, He says, *I was hungry, but you gave Me nothing to eat.* And how did he conclude? Thus: *They will go to eternal fire, but the righteous to eternal life* (Matthew 25:46). (*Sermon* 137)[27]

In this single quotation we have a powerful, if homey, statement of the Augustinian teaching on the Mystical Body and on the importance of practical charitable work. In many of these statements he speaks about serving Christ, but I do not recall any statement of a mystic sort where he saw Christ or had an experience of Christ serving the poor. There are such experiences in later spiritual writings, in the legend of St. Martin of Tours and especially in the life of St. Francis. These experiences, of which we have only secondary descriptions written by others, may be a linking of the ecstatic love of God and the works of charity. But if Augustine had such experiences he does not appear to have written about them.

(3) *How Does Union with the Church by Works of Charity Relate to Union with God?* I answer my third question by saying that in this life the works of charity done in the unity of the Mystical Body are instrumental for Augustine. They move us along the road to heaven and may indeed help us in many ways both to experience and to grow in the love of Christ. We come to God in fact by allowing Christ to work in us as he cares for his own members through our works of charity. This charity is fed by the Holy Spirit through the sacraments and life of the church, that is, the *Templum Dei*. The church as we see in the *Homily on Psalm 41* is filled with sweet music—the examples of the saints.

But we should not let these beautiful words on the Mystical Body and on charity to the brethren make us think that Augustine was unrealistic about the church on earth. Like St. Paul, he suffered much for the church and from the church. His life as a bishop was filled with disputes. He was often in personal controversies with other Catholic Christians, not the least of whom was Jerome. His sermons often contained sharp words for the men of Hippo. He had trouble with the community of men he had established, and the convent he started fell apart before his death.[28]

Because of the limitations of an introduction, we have not been able to cite all pertinent quotations from Augustine on the mystical experience.[29]

There are several important aspects in the spirituality of St. Augustine that are not covered in this chapter. His teaching on the central spiritual task of restoring the image of the Trinity in the soul and the relation of the Trinity to the individual believer will be taken up in chapter 5 on Augustine as the theologian of the Trinity. The more practical aspects of the spiritual life—especially the writings on love and prayer—will be covered in chapter 7 on Augustine as a spiritual guide.

Seeking Christ by Serving the Church—
Even to Martydom

As I looked for a passage to close this chapter, I came across a later *Sermon* of St. Augustine on the Gospel of St. John (*Sermon* 123 on John 21:15-19) that brings together Augustine's teaching on purity of heart, love of Jesus Christ, and love of the flock of Christ. It may not say it all, but when you recall that Augustine had to encourage the bishops of Africa to stay with their flocks as the Vandals advanced with pillage and death, the sermon takes on a very realistic quality. Had Augustine lived another year he might well have been a martyr himself when Hippo was sacked and burned. Speaking very powerfully of the martyr's death he writes:

The vice which those who feed Christ's sheep have to guard themselves against most of all is seeking their own interests instead of those of Jesus Christ, and using those for whom Christ's blood was shed to further their own ambitions. In those who feed his sheep, the love of Christ should grow to such great spiritual ardor as to conquer even the natural fear of death, which makes us unwilling to die even when we wish to live with Christ. Even the apostle Paul says he longs to depart and be with Christ (Philippians 1:23), yet he laments in deep distress, wishing not to be stripped but rather additionally clothed, so that his mortal body might be absorbed by immortal life (2 Corinthians 5:4-5).

And so Our Lord said to the disciple whom he knew loved him, *When you are old, you will stretch out your arms, and another will gird you and lead you where you do not wish to go. And he told him this to indicate the death by which he would glorify God* (John 21:18-19). *You will stretch out your arms,* he says—that is, you will be crucified. But to come to this, *another will gird you and lead you,* not where you wish to go, but *where you do not wish to go.* He told him first what would happen, then how it would happen, for it was not when he had been crucified, but when he was on his way to be crucified, that he was led where he did not wish to go; after his crucifixion he went away, not where he did not wish to go, but rather where he did wish to go. Of course, when he was released from the body he wished to be with Christ, but if it had been possible he would have desired eternal life without the trouble of death, to which trouble he was led unwillingly, but out of which he was led willingly. He went to his death unwillingly, but he willingly conquered it, and so he abandoned that feeling of weakness which makes no one want to die, but which is so natural that not even old age could remove it from blessed Peter, who was told, *When you are old,* you will be led *where you do not wish to go.*

For our consolation, our Savior transformed this feeling even in himself, saying, *Father, if possible, let this cup pass from me* (Matthew 26:39), since he had certainly come to die, was not compelled to die but chose to, and by his own power was to lay down his life and by his own power take it again. But whatever the trouble of death, the power of love must conquer it, the love with which he is loved who, since he is our life, was willing to endure even death for us. If we had no trouble, not even a little, in dying, the glory of the martyrs would not be so great. But if the good shepherd, who laid down his life for his sheep, made so many of those sheep martyrs for himself, how much more must those to whom he entrusts the feeding of his sheep—that is, the teaching and guiding of them—fight to the death for truth and against sin?

Therefore, with the example of his passion set before us, who cannot see that shepherds must rather cling to the shepherd by following his example, if many of the sheep have also followed his example. . . . He has indeed made all his sheep, for all of whom he died, for he too was made a sheep, so that he might die for all.[30]

Chapter Five

Augustine—Theologian of the Trinity

When one is touring the Alps or the Rockies or just looking at a picture, one is likely to be disappointed that there is no single great peak, no top of the world, so to speak, that stands out. The highest peaks are surrounded by others only a few dozen feet lower. On the other hand if you visit the Pacific Northwest you will come across great peaks standing all by themselves, rising abruptly out of the plains, like Mount Rainier or Mount Hood. Their solitude makes them all the more impressive. There is one of these solitary peaks that stands about over all the rest. In fact when I first saw it from a plane and flew right over its great glacier shining in the bright African sun I realized that I had never seen a mountain quite as impressive as Kilimanjaro, a name that aptly means the "mountain of God." Symbolically, we step a bit away from our Alps to Augustine's mountain of God, which has been until recently a forgotten and remote mountain, his great masterwork along with the *Confessions* and *The City of God*, *The Trinity*.

I must be clear in stating that he is not *the* theologian of the Trinity, but one of the theologians of the Trinity, although in his own unique way. He is in debt to very early Western Christian writers like Justin Martyr, Irenaeus, and Tertullian; and, like every writer on the Trinity after the Council of Nicea, he must in many ways be beholden to the intrepid archbishop of Alexandria, Athanasius. Augustine read the great Greek father Gregory Nazianzen and Didymus the Blind and possibly Basil and Epiphanius.[1] It is beyond the scope of this introduction, but if you are interested, Fr. Hill and Dr. McGinn will provide you with many

insights into Arianism and the post–Arian controversies. A forgotten classic rarely mentioned and excellent for background is
Cardinal Newman's illuminating gem *The Arians.*[2]

De Trinitate — The Book

The work in question, *De Trinitate* (*The Trinity*), had a remarkable
and bumpy history, unlike the *Confessions*. In the covering letter
to Bishop Aurelius of Carthage, Augustine indicates its composition had been a long task, begun when he was fairly young (forty-
six years old) around the year 400 and not finished until shortly
after 420. When he was a bit more than half finished certain
admirers got hold of the incomplete manuscript and published it
without his knowledge or consent. He was most annoyed,
undoubtedly because he had not even had the time to correct
what he had written. In response, he discontinued this book for a
long time. Aurelius and others prevailed upon him to complete
the work, which the experts say has some rough spots because of
its strange history. The person looking for spiritual reading must
know that the task set forth by this book is totally intellectual but
that the tone is deeply spiritual and to borrow Fr. Hill's enlightening adjective, "dramatic." Hill calls *The Trinity* a "dramatic history of God"—not God's own history because God is absolute
and unchanging, but the history of his revelation of himself especially in the creation and redemption of the human race. Much of
the high drama is in the struggle of believing Christians to find
the image of the Trinity in themselves. This search is justified by
the mysterious words of Genesis 1:26: "Let us make man in our
image," and the spirituality of St. Paul, which calls us to be
renewed and put on the new man created according to God in the
justice and the holiness of truth (Ephesians 4:23). The image of
God (*imago Dei*) and its essential importance in understanding
the spiritual task of the disciple of Christ are the subject of this
book. Therefore, although *The Trinity* is a work of the mind, it is a
profound spiritual document. Goulvan Madec, in *Augustine of
Hippo,* states with much authority that "every word by Augustine
is essentially spiritual" unless it was written in a theological con-

troversy.[3] Doctor McGinn sums up the goal of *The Trinity* succinctly:

> Augustine's purpose in writing *The Trinity* was to make his readers conscious that it is the unalterable trinitarian nature of their inner being that makes possible attaining full and perfect vision of the Trinity. This long and difficult text is an invitation to open the interior eye to the triune God already present and active within, and thus to attain vision through the conscious appropriation of the *imago Trinitatis*. This is why Augustine insists that the introspective activity involved in our personal recognition of the trinity within our own consciousness is not meant to be a pure mental exercise in and of itself—it is intended to lead the soul to that participation in divine Wisdom which is not just the recognition that the *mens* does indeed bear the image of the Trinity, but also the conviction that the whole purpose for which this image was created was to attune itself more consciously and more directly to its heavenly source: "Hence this trinity of the mind is not on that account the image of God because the mind remembers itself, understands itself, and loves itself, but because it can also remember, understand and love him by whom it was made. And when it does so, it becomes wise; but if it does not, even though it remembers itself, knows itself, and loves itself, it is foolish." (*The Trinity* 14.12.15)[4]

The structure of *The Trinity* is, according to the insight of Fr. Hill, somewhat similar to the slope of a mountain peak (my image). Out of fifteen short books, the first seven are basically a review and exploration of the Catholic belief of the Trinity. Book 1 is a dogmatic statement of the mystery. Then books 2–4 examine the scriptural foundation of this belief with special emphasis on the "missions" or the sending of the Son and the Holy Spirit. Books 5–7 are an application of reason to the revelation of the Trinity logically enough following on the statement of revelation filling out one of Augustine's very basic principles, "Unless you believe, you will not understand" (from the Septuagint, or early Greek version of Isaiah 7:9).

Book 8 is the peak, so to speak, of *The Trinity*, but it is an uneven peak as we shall see. Augustine states in the introduction in the book that he intends to go over the things he has written so far in a more involved method of approach. In this book

Augustine uses truth and goodness as the bridge between the divine mystery (which in itself we can never experience) and the relative mystery of the human person. Immediately we suspect that *The Trinity* is going to take a strong psychological bent, and it does. This, perhaps, is why this book, which received little attention in the past, is having a revival of interest in our own psychologically focused time. In books 9–11 Augustine constructs theoretical models of mental operations with the hope that they will provide images of the relationships in the Trinity, literally images of God. In book 10 the image is finally seen to consist in the co-equal and really distinct acts of inner self or mind when it remembers itself, understands itself or wills or loves itself, to use Fr. Hill's succinct summary. The terms "co-equal," "consubstantial," and "distinct" are borrowed from the Council of Nicea's dogmatic definition of the Trinity.[5]

It is very important, if you were a student of the old catechism, to note that Augustine does not say that the image is memory, intellect, and will, but rather the mind's operations of its own self-directed love toward self. The mistaken notion that Augustine taught that memory, intellect, and will (which are not co-equal or ever really seen as distinct in modern psychology but rather different functions of the same psyche) are images of the Trinity is traceable to Peter Lombard, a medieval theologian, who was in my estimation not much of a psychologist at all.[6] Augustine then in book 12 beautifully restudies salvation history (the fall and redemption) in the light of this new construct of the activities or functions of the mind. Of special importance to us is his view of contemplation (wisdom) in book 14. This is the process of conversion by which the individual believer finally becomes part of the drama of salvation by the deepest personal involvement, that is, conversion through charity and purity of heart.

Book 15 is the final dramatic bombshell, the last act, as it were, where Augustine tells us that this beautiful image or analogy is totally inadequate as a representation of the Trinity. Some find this a bit of a disappointment, but I love it and, being a devotee of mystery, I cannot keep a straight face while I read this critique of all he has done. For all eternity we will be learning things about the mystery of the Godhead and then moving on to deeper understandings because all revelation, though true, will be incomplete. This Kilimanjaro leads to an endless series of higher peaks, to bright days with no sunset, where without effort we shall rest while moving on.

O Lord God, grant us peace, for Thou hast granted us all things, the peace of repose, the peace of Thy sabbath, the peace that has no evening. For this gloriously beautiful order of things that are very good will pass away when it has achieved its end: it will have its morning and its evening.

But the seventh day is without evening. It has no sunset, for You sanctified it that it may abide forever. After all Your works which were very good, You rested on the seventh day—although You made them with no interruption of Your repose. And likewise the voice of Your book tells us that we also, after our works—which are only very good because You have granted us to accomplish them—will rest in You in the Sabbath of life everlasting. (*Conf.* 13.35–37)

The Tools for Climbing to *The Trinity*

If you are already a little intimidated by this great work a very good way for you to make a relatively easy start after completing this brief introduction is to read Sr. Clark's gentle translations of books 8 and 14. We have indicated already that these are the key parts of this work. Her brief introductory note is helpful but you should reread the whole introduction to the volume again. You may be tempted to feel like you have gone to the summit of our mountain by cable car, but the fact is you have only had a quick view. Father Hill's erudite and readable explanations and insights fit well with his translation, which is more theological and probably a bit more literal. This translation will take you through the whole work.[7]

Doctor McGinn's analysis, although brief, takes up some issues that the others seem not to explore. He in fact helpfully stresses the practical application of the image-of-God analogy to the spiritual life. We will again gratefully borrow from his insights in this chapter and the last.

The following selections are not meant to present a summary of the Augustinian exploration of the doctrine of the Trinity. They are to provide glimpses of the work. I hope they will thrill you enough to make you read *The Trinity* as the sights of Kilimanjaro lifted me up years ago. As you see, we will use some citations from Fr. Hill's translation and others from Sr. Clark's.

Why and How We Try to Explain Revealed Truth about God

The following passage gives Augustine's reason for writing and with it a warning about the limitation of these explanations. He will return to this theme at the end of the book.

The divine scriptures then are in the habit of making something like children's toys out of things that occur in creation, by which to entice our sickly gaze and get us step by step to seek as best we can the things that are above and forsake the things that are below. Things, however, that are peculiar to God and do not occur anywhere in creation are rarely mentioned by sacred scripture. . . .

So then it is difficult to contemplate and have full knowledge of God's substance, which without any change in itself makes things that change, and without any passage of time in itself creates things that exist in time. That is why it is necessary for our minds to be purified before that inexpressible reality can be inexpressibly seen by them; and in order to make us fit and capable of grasping it, we are led along more endurable routes, nurtured on faith as long as we have not yet been endowed with that necessary purification. . . .

That is why, with the help of the Lord our God, we shall undertake to the best of our ability to give them the reasons they clamor for, and to account for the one and only and true God being a trinity, and for the rightness of saying, believing, understanding that the

Father and the Son and the Holy Spirit are of one and the same substance or essence. (*The Trinity* 1.2–4)[8]

God Is Truth and Goodness

Something needs to be said here about the statements we are about to read, for instance, "God is truth." Usually in our customary way of speaking this statement means, "it is true that there is a God," or even, "what God reveals about himself is true." This is an instrumental way of speaking; messages that are correlated accurately with reality are called true and communicate true information or truth. This is not what the words mean when St. Augustine writes: "God is truth," or Jesus says: "I am the way, the truth, and the life." The first way of speaking instrumentally is, to my way of thinking, more Aristotelian, which means that accurate messages are the causes of our knowing what is true. You probably grew up thinking this way. I suspect that I was drawn to St. Augustine at the age of fourteen because, for reasons I do not understand, I did not think like an Aristotelian but like what is generally called a Platonist. I have never seen these two approaches to true knowledge as contradictory, but certainly they are contrasting. It is important for you to appreciate this second way of thinking if you are going to appreciate Augustine's mind in *The Trinity* and many other works: "God is truth, goodness, beauty, or even light and love."

Another Way of Thinking

Permit me to use a little self-reference to illustrate this. When I was only in mid-elementary school, a decade old, my grandmother use to take my cousin, my brother, and me on trips to the cultural sights in New York City. Although my father was a construction engineer and eventually built some of the great cultural buildings in New York City at Lincoln Center, I had little or no interest in architecture and even less in engineering. I loved the paintings and statues in the Metropolitan Museum of Art and in the Cloisters and the classical music at the Music Hall. It could be medieval paintings of Christ at Calvary or the flowers of Van Gogh. I had a powerful experience of beauty and not only of something beautiful. I was far less interested in the technique that I could admire—and still do—though I was in a nameless but familiar way intrigued and even entranced by an inner something that had no name. It might be caused by a painting of Blessed Angelico or Turner or Chagall; Gregorian chant, Mozart, or Rachmaninoff, or even some country folk hymns like "I Wonder as I Wander." It could have been the darkness under the arches of St. Patrick's Cathedral or the coming of the summer thunderstorms, the face of some little baby or of a venerable old nun, or even a young couple smiling gently and holding hands as they walked by. I did not know what this was but Plato and St. Augustine gave it a name—it was beauty itself and not simply something beautiful. It was there before anyone sang or played or painted it. It was more than mere sentiment as in the movie *Lassie* or *Mrs. Miniver.* It was more than nobility as found in films like *Joan of Arc* or charity in *Monsieur Vincent* (a life of St. Vincent de Paul). I finally found some people who also knew what it was— among them St. Augustine and St. Francis. Augustine could speak of it as truth or goodness or beauty; they were really not so different I thought. Francis could be enraptured by this penetrating and pervasive reality—really a presence—and he spoke to me by his life rather than by his simple and gentle words, although his "Song of Brother Sun" echoed around me whenever I went into the woods or the mountains. He could be drawn to it with tears when he wept over glowing icons of the cross. Whether it was heard or seen in nature or art or in certain relationships it was the same thing; it was beauty or goodness or truth.

There are many people who think and experience reality in this way. Some are educated; some are very plain; some are good and are drawn to the true and good; some are quite wicked and do not simply do evil things, they pursue evil because of its perversity. When I ran into the French writer Genet, "the devil's saint," by accidently picking up his cynical and blasphemous book entitled *Our Lady of the Flowers,* I knew in a few paragraphs that this man sought evil and ugliness as I ran after truth and beauty. His pursuit was not for good but for the state that is the absence of good. I prayed for Genet when he was still alive because anyone who can know evil in that way can also come to know the true and the good. I also saw this dark trait in the etchings of Aubrey Beardsley, who died repentant with the sacraments of the Church. There is an essential difference between the awareness of good and the awareness of evil; one leads to eternity and the other leads into everlasting frustration and hopelessness. Those who pursue evil eventually learn the truth of Augustine's words in the *Soliloquies*, that evil is ultimately nothing at all.

Often when I read theological writings about books like the *Confessions* or *The Trinity* and the writer is analyzing what truth means in a line like "Where have you not walked with me, O Truth" (*Conf.* 10.10), I have wondered how anyone could dissect such words. Shall someone analyze "O Beauty, so ancient and yet so new"? Or even, "I am the way and the truth"? Is not intuition and silence and the mysterious expression of certitude (of truth) or delight (of beauty) itself something mysterious that makes human experience much more real than any brilliant analysis? When it comes to the knowledge of God, Augustine says: "Eye has not seen it, for it has no color; ear has not heard it, for it makes no sound. It has not entered into the human heart because our hearts must enter into it."[9]

This truth and beauty and goodness as aspects of absolute reality are beyond our direct experience, but we can, at times, catch a fleeting glimpse of their presence. I am not saying that this way of thinking is a superior or a more spiritual way of experiencing things than the more instrumental. Saint Thomas, that great baptizer of Aristotelian thought, was a saint. Genet was quite the opposite. Plato was a great philosopher (but not a saint) because he enunciated early in human intellectual history this way of experiencing reality beyond what is perceived by the senses. For the moment, even if you do not think this way, you might try it for a better understanding of the next few citations.

The Equal Truth and Goodness
of the Three Persons

We affirm that two or three Persons in this Trinity are not a greater reality than any one of them. Our material way of thinking goes against our grasping this for the simple reason that although it is aware according to its capacity of the truly existing realities which were created, it cannot perceive Truth itself which has created them. If it could perceive Truth, the fact previously affirmed would be as clear as daylight. Only Truth itself has true being: There is nothing greater in substance except that which more truly is. But there cannot be degrees of truth in the sphere of the spiritual and the changeless, for in that sphere everything is equally changeless and eternal. . . .

But Father and Son together have no more true being than the Father alone or the Son alone. Both together, therefore, are no greater reality than either of them alone. And since the Holy Spirit exists no less truly, neither are Father and Son together a greater reality than the Spirit, because they are not a reality existing more truly.

. . . Behold, if you can, you a soul weighed down by many and various earthly thoughts, behold and see, if you can that God is Truth. It is written, "God is Light" (1 Jn 1:5)—not the light seen by our eyes but that seen by the heart upon hearing the words "He is Truth." Ask not: What is Truth? Immediately there will arise the mists of sensible images, thick clouds of phantasms darkening that clear empyrean which shone forth momentarily upon your sight at that word "Truth." At that moment, hold fast—if possible— that flash of vision that touches you with the word "Truth." (*The Trinity* 8.1)[10]

Goodness, like truth and beauty, are according to Plato transcendent qualities of being, and consequently according to Augustine, guided by Scripture, aspects of the absolute being of God.

Goodness and Love

In a passage that follows shortly on the one just above, Augustine turns our attention to the good and the way we arrive at possession of the good through love.

Try again and think of it this way. Only what is good attracts your love. The earth with its high mountains, gentle hills, level plains is good. The lovely and fertile land is good; the sturdy house with its proportions, its spaciousness and light is good. The bodies of living things are good; the mild and healthy air is good; pleasurable and health-giving food is good; health itself, a freedom from pain and exhaustion, is good. The human face with its symmetrical features, its glad countenance, its high coloring is good; the heart of a friend whose companionship is sweet and whose love is loyal is good; a righteous man is good; wealth for what it enables us to do is good; the sky with its sun, moon, and stars is good; the angels by their holy obedience are good; speech which teaches persuasively and counsels suitably is good; the poem of musical rhythm and profound meaning is good.

But enough! This is good and that is good; take away "this" and "that" and gaze if you can upon good itself: Then you will behold God, good not through the having of any other good thing, but He is the goodness of every good. For we could not affirm by a true judgement that any one of those good things I have cited (or others you may see or think of) is better than another if in our mind there were not imprinted the idea of good itself as the standard by which we either approve or prefer. So our love must rise to God as the Good itself, not in the way we love this or that good thing. The soul has to seek that Good over which it does not act as judge in some superior way but to which it will cleave in love. And what is that Good but God?—not the good soul, the good angel, the good heavens, but the good Good! (*The Trinity* 8.3; trans. Clark)

It must be obvious that none of us on earth has come to the complete possession of the good and consequently to blessedness. We have, according to Augustine, a fleeting glance or experience here and there. What tells us of goodness or truth or beauty if we do not have possession of them yet? The answer is faith, and the means of possession is a loving and pure heart.

Faith, Hope, Love and a Pure Heart

But we have to remain steadfast in that Good by love and cleave to it, so that we may enjoy the presence of Him from whom we have our being, and whose absence would make it impossible for us to be at all. "We walk by faith as yet, and not by sight" (2 Cor 5:7). We do not yet see God, as the same Apostle says, "face to face" (1 Cor 13:12). But unless we now love Him, we shall never see Him. . . .

God is seen and apprehended as far as He can be by the pure in heart; they, we read, are "happy, for they shall see God" (Mt 5:8). Before we are strengthened to see Him there can be no purifying of the heart to see Him unless He is loved in faith. Faith, hope and charity, those three virtues which the whole structure of the Bible exists to build up, are only in the soul which believes what it does not yet see, and hopes for and loves what it believes. Therefore if He is believed in, there is already love even of Him who is not yet known. (*The Trinity* 8.4)

After discussions of imaginative images of our Lord, our Lady, and St. Paul (which images are really of small importance), Augustine makes the point that we must be sure that we are worshiping the true God, not a false one whom we happen to call by the name Trinity. He is emphatic in saying that when we love someone it must not be for their appearance but for their righteousness. We should have a proper self-love for the same reason (*The Trinity* 7.10). Then he makes clear that the test of whether we love God is whether we love our neighbor with a true love.

Love of Neighbor and Love of God

Such statements, (Rom. 8:28; 5:5) imply that whoever loves God should do what God has commanded, that one's love depends upon one's doing, and thus one must also love one's neighbor because God has commanded this. At times Scripture discusses only the love of neighbor. "Bear you one another's burdens and so you shall fulfill the law of Christ" (Gal 6:2). "The whole Law is fulfilled in one saying, namely, you shall love your neighbor as yourself" (Gal 5:14). Or, as in the Gospel, "Whatsoever you would that men should do unto you, even so do unto them; for this is the Law and the Prophets" (Mt 7:12). In many other places in Holy Scripture the love of neighbor alone seems to be advocated for our perfection and nothing is mentioned about the love of God, although the Law and the Prophets depend upon both command-ments. This is because one who loves his neighbor must neces-sarily first have the love for Love itself. But "God is Love, and he who abides in Love, abides in God" (1 Jn 4:16). Consequently, first one must love God above all things. . . .

Let no one say: "I do not know what I am to love." Let him love his brother, and he will love that same love; he knows the love whereby he loves better than he knows the brother whom he loves. God can be more known to him than his brother, really more known because more present; more known because more interior; more known because more certain. Embrace the love that is God; through love embrace God. He is the very love that joins together in holy bond all good angels and all God's servants, uniting them and us to one another in subjection to Himself. The more cleansed we are from the swelling of pride, the more we are filled with love; and is not whoever is filled with love filled with God? (*The Trinity* 8.7; trans. Clark)

There is another element that is necessary for the Christian's love of God and neighbor. Augustine lived in a time when people sought by various cults to have control of cosmic powers and to do various signs. We would call these paranormal phenomena today, and they are much the rage at the far side of that vague thing called the New Age. Sometimes they are also given undue attention by Christians.[11] Augustine comments: "Those who search for God by means of such powers placed over the world or its parts fall far away from Him, separated not by space but by opposing affections. They do not seek a reverent surrender which obtains the peace of God."[12] He continues:

So when the Lord Jesus Christ Himself performed miracles, He tried to give a fuller truth to the astonished spectators, to convert them from their immersion in temporal signs to interior and eter-nal realities. "Come unto me, all you that labor and are heavily burdened, and I will 'refresh you,' take my yoke upon you" (Mt. 11:28). He does not say, "Learn of me, for I raise up them that have been dead four days"; but "Learn of me, for I am meek and lowly of heart" (Mt. 11:29). The firm ground of humility is stronger and safer than any wind-swept elevation, so He continues, "and you shall find rest for your souls." For "Love is not puffed up" (1 Cor 13:4); "God is love" (1 Jn 4:8); "The faithful in love shall rest in him" (Wis 3:9), summoned from the noise-filled external world to joyful silence. (*The Trinity* 8.7,11; trans. Clark)

The First Image

In the following passage on love, for the first time Augustine begins to arrive at an answer to the question that he began with, namely, "What is the image of God and the human soul?" Here at the very end of book 8 he discovers the image—the lover, that which is loved, and love itself. He does not say that this is the image of the Trinity in the soul, but rather he indicates that it is a place to look.

Now what is love or charity which is praised and preached so highly by divine Scripture except the love of the Good? Love is the activity of a lover and it has a definite object. There we have three things: the lover, that which is loved, and love. Love itself is only a kind of life which unites together or tries to unite two beings, the lover and the beloved. This is the case in the carnal loves of the external world; but let us leave the body and ascend to the soul where we may drink of a purer and clearer source. What does the soul love in a friend except the soul? Even here there are three: the lover, the beloved and love.

There still remains for us a further ascent from here to seek those higher things as far as this is possible to man. But here we may pause, not asserting that we have discovered what we were seeking, but as having discovered, as seekers do, the place to look. We have discovered, not the reality itself, but where it is to be sought. And that will suffice to provide a point from which a fresh start may be made. (*The Trinity* 8.10; trans. Clark)

A Second and Better Image

In book 9, which is just six pages long in Fr. Hill's translation, Augustine perfects his first image of the Trinity, love. Let me put it rather simplistically. He sees that the image of the lover, the loved, and love is not perfectly apt for the Trinity because it brings the lover out of self and could describe any sort of love. He then moves to a psychological analysis of the mind's own knowledge and love of itself, what we might today call a self-concept and self-esteem. This is ultimately the image that Augustine will settle on as an analogue of the image of the Trinity in the soul. It is not the Trinity but a reflection or image, and in the last book we will find out how inadequate this analogue is. We might think that this image is an improvement over St. Patrick's legendary use of the shamrock or the three-leaf clover to help the tribes of Erin to grasp the Trinity, but in relation to the reality of God it is also just a shadow.

In a well-ordered human mind relating to self (and for the moment not relating to others), Augustine sees three somethings. The following passage is one out of several where Augustine explains the well-ordered mind as an image of the Trinity. Speaking of the mind (we would say, of the psyche) he writes:

Just as you have two somethings, mind and its love, when it loves itself, so you have two somethings, mind and its knowledge, when it knows itself. The mind therefore and its love and knowledge are three somethings, and these three are one thing, and when they are complete they are equal.

But they are in each other too, because the mind loving is in love, and love is in the knowledge of the lover, and knowledge is in the mind knowing. They are each in the other two, because the mind which knows and loves itself is in its love and knowledge, and the love of the mind loving and knowing itself is in the mind and its knowledge, and the knowledge of the mind knowing and loving itself is in the mind and its love, because it loves itself knowing and knows itself loving.

But with these three, when mind knows and loves itself the trinity remains of mind, love, knowledge. Nor are they jumbled up together in any kind of mixture, though they are each one in itself and each whole in their total, whether each in the other two or the other two in each, in any case all in all. (*The Trinity* 9.4, 8; trans. Hill)

Thus St. Augustine sees mind, knowledge, and love and their interrelationships as an analogy of the co-equal, consubstantial Trinity. Mind represents the Father or the divine origin; the Word (which means knowledge in Greek) represents the Son; and Love, the Holy Spirit. There is a great deal more written, and I recommend Fr. Hill's translation for clarity. Books 9–11 are mostly psychological, and books 12–14 mostly historical and scriptural. In all of these St. Augustine analyzes, refines, and justifies his image. I suggest that you get to know Augustine a bit more before you climb up these cliffs and crevices to the peak of the mountain. However, book 14 will help you to gain some foothold for the spiritual life from this explanation.

In a few words, Sr. Clark deftly summarizes book 14:

> In Book XIV, we find the culmination of the spiritual life to be the soul's participation in Divine Wisdom wherein God Himself is the object of the mind's memory, understanding, and will. If God has made us toward Himself, then our hearts will be restless until they rest in Him. Therefore the spiritual life embraces both time and eternity. The one reality that is present here below and will forever continue is that of charity, which requires the presence of God and our awareness of God as Love. Through the gift of charity, or Grace, God unites people together and as a temple or sacred city they are a dwelling place of the Trinity—God in whose likeness they grow in the measure of their love.[13]

Augustine begins by introducing the idea of wisdom, the supreme wisdom of God himself and the worship of God, which is wisdom for men. Augustine recalls that the ancient philosophers, following Pythagoras, dared not to identify themselves as wise men but only as lovers of wisdom. Augustine then proceeds to review what he has said in this long book and takes up questions that he cannot adequately answer. For instance, is the mind of a small child an image of the Trinity? About all his previous discussions he finally concludes: "Here therefore is the mind remembering itself, understanding itself and loving itself. Perceiving this we perceive a trinity, a trinity far less than God but finally an image of God" (*The Trinity* 14.12; trans. Clark).

But this is not enough for the person of faith. It is an image, that is all. I must say, however, that it is an improvement over the shamrock.

The Mind Must Worship the Triune God

Now this trinity of the mind is the image of God, not because the mind remembers, understands, and loves itself, but because it also has the power to remember, understand, and love its Maker. And in doing this it attains wisdom. If it does not do this, the memory, understanding, and love of itself is no more than an act of folly. Therefore, let the mind remember its God, to whose image it was made, let it understand and love him.

In brief, let it worship the uncreated God who created it with the capacity for Himself, and in whom in can be made partaker. Hence it is written: "Behold, the worship of God is wisdom" (Jb 28:28). By participating in that supreme Light wisdom will belong to the mind not by its own light, and it will reign in bliss only where the eternal Light is. (*The Trinity* 14.12; trans. Clark)

Unfortunately, the human mind is corrupted by sin, original sin and actual sin. This corruption can only be taken away by the one mediator between the human race and God, Jesus Christ. A self-love that is distorted has severely obscured the image of God in the soul.

The Mind Set Right

For the mind's self-love becomes right instead of evil when it loves God by partaking of whom the image we mention not only exists but is transformed from old to new, from deformity to beauty, from unhappiness to happiness. The power of self-love is so strong that if a man has to choose he will lose all worldly things rather than lose himself. Only with God above, to whom the Psalmist sings "My strength will I keep safe with thee," and again, "Draw near unto Him, and be lightened," can a man secure his strength and enjoy the divine Light as his own. (*The Trinity* 14.14; trans. Clark)

As we have stated above in chapter 2, Augustine never assumed that a person, once converted, has been irrevocably saved. We must constantly work for reform and renewal.

The Restoration of the Image

Those moved by the reminder to convert again to the Lord from that state of deformity wherein worldly desires conformed them to this world have to receive from the Lord their reformation, as the Apostle says, "Be not conformed to this world, but be reformed in newness of your mind" (Rom 12:2), the beginning of the image's reforming must come from him who first formed it. It cannot of itself re-form the self which it could deform. The Apostle says in another place: "Be renewed in the spirit of your mind, and put on the new man, which has been created according to God in justice and holiness of truth" (Eph 4:23). The words "according to God" agree with what we read elsewhere: "to the image of God" (Gen 1:27). Justice and holiness of truth were lost through sin; hence this image became deformed and discolored. When the image is re-formed and renewed the mind receives what it once had. (*The Trinity* 14.16; trans. Clark)

The final destiny of the human being is eternal life when the image of God will be purified by the perfect vision of God. We will no longer see through a glass darkly.

The Perfect Vision of God in the Image

When the final day of life reveals a man, in the midst of this progress and growth, holding steadfast to the faith of the Mediator the holy angels will await him to bring him home to the God whom he has served and by whom he must be perfected; and at the end of the world he will receive an incorruptible body, not for punishment but for glory. For the likeness of God will be perfect in this image only in the perfect vision of God: of which vision the Apostle Paul says: "Now we see through a glass darkly, but then face-to-face" (1 Cor 13:12). And again: "But we with unveiled face beholding the glory of the Lord are transformed into the same image from glory to glory, as from the spirit of the Lord" (2 Cor 3:18). (*The Trinity* 16.17; trans. Clark)

In book 14 Augustine is very clear to state that the image of the Trinity in the soul is not such that one could deduce the doctrine of the Trinity from it. Thus, he clearly affirms the necessity of faith. Using 1 Corinthians 13:12, "We see now through a mirror in an enigma" (*per speculum in aenigmatate*), a literal translation wisely used by Fr. Hill, Augustine explains the inadequacies of this image. These discussions are very valuable for reinforcing our appreciation of transcendent mysteries and can be read with much profit after one is more familiar with Augustine.

In the style he found so successful thirty years earlier when he wrote the *Confessions,* Augustine brings this great work to a end with a soliloquy and then a prayer. These remarkably summarize the great work and leave us with a lasting image like a glance back at Kilimanjaro as our plane speeds onward. His prayer also includes a warning to himself and to his readers not to take his thoughts and images too seriously because the thoughts of men are vain (Ps. 94:11). He asks forgiveness for any mistakes that he has made. Here in Fr. Hill's translation is part of the last prayer:

O Lord our God, we believe in you, Father and Son and Holy Spirit. Truth would not have said, *Go and baptize the nations in the name of the Father and of the Son and of the Holy Spirit* (Mt 28:19), unless you were a triad. Nor would you have commanded us to be baptized, Lord God, in the name of any who is not Lord God. Nor would it have been said with divine authority, *Hear O Israel, the Lord your God is one God* (Dt 6:4), unless while being a triad you were still one Lord God. And if you, God and Father, were yourself also the Son your Word Jesus Christ, were yourself also your gift the Holy Spirit, we would not read in the documents of truth *God sent his Son* (Gal 4:4), nor would you, only-begotten one, have said of the Holy Spirit, *whom the Father will send in my name* (Jn 14:26), and, *whom I will send you from the Father* (Jn 15:26). Directing my attention toward this rule of faith as best I could, as far as you enabled me to, I have sought you and desired to see intellectually what I have believed, and I have argued much and toiled much. O Lord my God, my one hope, listen to me lest out of weariness I should stop wanting to seek you, but let me seek your face always, and with ardor. Do you yourself give me the strength to seek, having caused yourself to be found and having given me the hope of finding you more and more. Before you lies my strength and my weakness; preserve the one, heal the other. Before you lies my knowledge and my ignorance; where you have opened to me, receive me as I come in; where you have shut to me, open to me as I knock. Let me remember you, let me understand you, let me love you. Increase these things in me until you refashion me entirely. (*The Trinity* 15.53; trans Hill)

The reader may be wondering what practical thoughts for the spiritual life can be culled from this introduction to the great work on the Trinity. Do not go away simply with an appreciation of Augustine's intelligence. This is absolutely the last thing he wants you to do because he did not think that human intelligence was a way to God. His book is about faith, and then faith seeking understanding. His book is about truth, but truth itself, not arguments that are more or less true. When he uses these reasonings and arguments he always acknowledges their limitations. In fact, in book 15, he shows the reader the holes in his intellectual enterprise of finding an image of the Trinity. Augustine obviously builds on Scripture and revelation. This is his consistent method of operation. He also builds, as we have tried to indicate, with his unfamiliar use of truth, goodness, love, and beauty, which are to him more than simply words or philosophical terms. They do not merely indicate things that are more or less true or beautiful; but when opened to grace we are drawn by the power of truth and beauty itself. I attempted to illustrate this way of thinking, which Fr. Hill calls Platonic (I think the term is accurate but historically restrictive), by my own experience before I ever read a line of Plato. I draw this whole investigation of the Trinity to a conclusion with a warning. It is a warning against a purely intellectual pursuit of God given by one of the great minds of modern times, one who might be likely to be some day called the "Doctor of the Church." If Augustine were alive I believe that he would shout "Amen" to this most insightful passage of Cardinal Newman.

Truth has two attributes—beauty and power. . . . Pursue it, either as beauty or power, to its furthest extent and its true limit, and you are led by either road to the Eternal and Infinite, to the intimations of conscience and the announcements of the Church. Satisfy yourself with what is only visibly or intelligibly excellent, as you are likely to do, and you will make present utility and natural beauty the practical test of truth, and the sufficient object of the intellect. It is not that you at once reject Catholicism, but you will measure and proportion it by an earthly standard. You will throw its highest and most momentous disclosures into the background, you will deny its principles, explain away its doctrines, re-arrange its precepts, and make light of its practices, even while you profess it.

Knowledge, viewed as knowledge, exerts a subtle influence in throwing us back on ourselves, and making us our own centre, and our own minds the measure of all things. This is (its) tendency . . . to view Revealed Religion from an aspect of its own—to fuse and recast it—to tune it, as it were, to a different key, and to reset its harmonies—to circumscribe it by a circle which unwarrantably amputates here, and unduly develops there; and all under the notion, conscious or unconscious, that the human intellect, self-educated and self-supported, is more true and perfect in its ideas and judgments than that of Prophets and Apostles, to whom the sights and sounds of Heaven were immediately conveyed.[14]

Chapter Six

Augustine the Historian—
The City of God

Augustine never intended to be a great historian, and yet by writing *City of God* he provided the students of the ancient world with an immense library of information on the religious beliefs of his age—both Christian and pagan. What is more significant is that he wrote a philosophy of history that has influenced all serious approaches to this science, which is, in fact, the memory of the human race. Most important of all, Augustine proposed and, as it were, started the human race thinking about a universal society, a single family of human beings, and the elements necessary for the establishment of such a society. While I was working on this chapter, I attended an event sponsored by the Permanent Observer of the Holy See to the United Nations in Manhattan. The U.N. seems to many to be a failure, and certainly at times it fails because its only power is what the member states give to it; but the U.N. is also a hope, if you will, a dream; and the great human aspiration of a world society was in fact powerfully influenced by St. Augustine's *City of God*.[1] We will return to this most important aspect of *City of God*, the universal society, at the end of this chapter.

Augustine considered *City of God* his masterpiece, and yet for every thousand people who read the whole *Confessions* there are probably only a small handful who have ever read this massive work. Augustine spent fourteen years on *City of God* beginning when he was fifty-nine years of age and completing it when he was seventy-two, in 426, four years before his death. His reason for writing *City of God* was not proportionate either to the amount of labor involved or to the effect that the work has had on human thinking for the last fifteen hundred years. The circumstances of writing were very pragmatic; Augustine was seeking an answer to a problem of the church at that time. If he ever wondered about how long his book would be important to members of the church he might have thought his book had a life of a few decades at most. He had apparently no idea that he was writing a classic, a book for the ages, and so his work is filled with references, allusions, and great digressions most of which had relevance to hotly debated issues of the moment. On the other hand, when one reads the *Confessions,* one suspects that Augustine thought that the book might last for sometime as a work of Christian apologetics and spirituality. Along with addressing issues of the moment *City of God* casts light on overarching questions like redemption, original sin, and the possibility of a universal society and gives answers that would last through the ages.

The Origin of *City of God*

From the time of Constantine's Edict of Milan in 319 the process of the gradual christianizing of the classical world had begun. From then on most of the emperors and a growing number of state officials and nobles would be Christian and would show more or less deference to the Catholic or universal church. Paganism did not instantly disappear, however. Not only did it have a strong hold on the people living in the remote rural areas (*pagani* or "people of the countryside") but it also characterized a recognizable group of educated citizens who in one way or another held on to the old beliefs. The process of christianization had been going on for just about a hundred years when the barbarian chieftain Alaric sacked and pillaged the city of Rome in the year 410. Although both Christian and pagan writers had been denouncing the moral and cultural decline of the Roman civilization for two centuries, some literate pagans blamed the Christians and the church for this unthinkably shocking event. The two arguments they made were simple: first, the moral teachings of Christianity, especially on meekness and forgiveness of enemies, had undermined the strength of the people; and second, the pagan gods were punishing Rome for the gradual decline in sacrifices and for ending the official worship of these gods in the empire.

These were very serious arguments against the church and, although they seem far-fetched to us, they rang true to many who sought the return of the old ways and the old gods. In 412 the pagan writer Volusianus addressed these arguments against the new religion to Marcellinus, an important official in Africa, who was a Christian. Marcellinus in turn wrote to Augustine asking him to compose a defense of the church to exonerate it from the charge that it had brought this terrible calamity on Rome. Augustine began *City of God* to honor the request of Marcellinus and to take on the attackers of the church.

Augustine's response, put in the simplest way, was to point out that even pagan writers had been denouncing the decline of the empire in the centuries before the Edict of Milan and at a time when the persecuted church had no influence in the society. Second, Augustine pointed out, the pagan gods had never done anything to help anyone before, and, in fact, they were myths and not realities. The collapse of the moral virtues on which the early glory of the Roman state had been built was the root cause of its disastrous decline. The first ten books of *City of God* contain arguments against pagan religion and spell out the details of pagan religion. They provide historians with very comprehensive information on this subject. Augustine also gave many details of Christian life and practice and overall provided a valuable picture of the empire in decline.

Toward the end of book 10, Augustine begins to present his world vision of Christianity in contrast to paganism. He becomes an apologist and leaves behind the task presented to him by Marcellinus. In books 11–22 he moves from the discussion of Rome to the presentation of spirituality on a cosmic level. The real conflict is not between Rome and the barbarians but between the city of God and the city of evil. To the first city belong the good angels and those human beings who are turned toward God, and to the second city belong angels and men who are turned away from God. It is clear that from a spiritual and psychological point of view, the division of the two cities is one of will or desire and, in the language of our times, they are cities divided by values and goals chosen by human beings who are more or less free and responsible. In Augustine's more powerful language they are cities divided by two contradictory loves: the first, the heavenly city, is the society of God, good angels, and human beings directed to the desire for truth and goodness; the second, or earthly city, is made up of fallen angels and people of ill will who love only the passing things of the world. Vernon Burke sums up this great division so well in a single sentence, "All human history and culture may be viewed as the interplay of the competing values of these two loves and these two cities."[2]

Augustine was not a simplistic person by any means. Not only did he acknowledge the existence of good and bad angels—he calls these mysterious beings "celestial citizens"—but he also recognized that among those called Christians there are good and bad. The battle between these two cities is obviously fought in each individual human life—a constant reconversion toward God after greater or lesser turns toward the goals of the earthly city.

Can *City of God* Be Spiritual Reading?

In this short introduction to St. Augustine's works we are focusing on what may be helpful for those who wish to do spiritual reading, that is, reading that is edifying and instructs individuals and helps them toward progress on their journey to God. It must be admitted that this goal narrows our vision of a work like *City of God*. It will seem to some well-informed students of Augustine that such an approach to this work is basically unsatisfactory and does not do the work justice. But the goal of our introduction is precisely this: to introduce readers to the writings of Augustine, literally to *lead* them in (*intro ducere*); and so with this apology we will begin to cull some of the great and valuable ideas of this monumental work.

To return to our analogy of the Augustinian Alps, this work is a vast valley, filled with glens and peaks, caves and crevices. In fact, all we can do is to pause for a brief moment to survey this complex terrain, pick out the principal landmarks, and move on, hoping to return for a much longer visit.

Among the ideas of *City of God* likely to make the strongest impression on the reader are the following: God's providence, the desire for good (the foundation of moral behavior), the meaning of salvation and the Incarnation and God's mercy upon the fallen world, the possibilities of a virtuous society, the final outcome of the drama of humanity. These topics do not represent a summary of *City of God* but rather a selection of some of its key ideas most pertinent to readers whose goal is to expand and deepen their Christian moral values.

Providence

The ancient Greco-Roman world tended to see history in a fatalistic way, with human beings as helpless pawns in a game controlled either by the capricious gods or by the relentless cycle of history that constantly repeated itself. Such a vision either denies human freedom or, in the view of the more noble writers, pitted human beings against the tides of faith. Many historians were merely narrators of history and avoided making any larger sense of the chain of events, leaving the readers to form their own philosophy of history.

Augustine grasped that the Bible, beginning with the creation narrative in Genesis, presented history not as a fatalistic cycle but as a dramatic interaction of God with his intelligent creation, angels and human beings. History had a purpose, or better still, the study of history sought to identify in the apparent tangled scheme of events the great plan of God, which required the free response of his intelligent creatures to his call to share forever in his mysterious eternity. This idea of an all-powerful and all-knowing providence is clearly taught by Christ in the Gospels— where no sparrow falls to earth unknown and where the very moments of one's life are numbered. Christ not only taught that there is an overarching divine providence but that his followers must adhere to this and trust this providence even in the worst of circumstances, even in death.

Providence Versus Fate and Astrology

In the following citation from *City of God*, St. Augustine takes on the fatalists as well as those who believe in astrology. Incredibly, this belief in the power of stars to determine history still survives and makes an impact on the daily press.

The cause, then, of the greatness of the Roman Empire was neither fortune nor fate. (I am using these words in the sense of those who say or think that fortune, or chance, is what happens without cause or rational explanation, and that fate is what is bound to happen, in spite even of the will of God or of men.) On the contrary, Divine Providence alone explains the establishment of kingdoms among men. As for those who speak of fate, but mean by fate the will and power of God, they should keep their conception but change their expression. Surely, though, it is best to say at once what one will have to say as soon as one is asked what is meant by fate. Ordinarily, when people hear the word fate they think of nothing but the position of the stars at the moment of one's birth or conception. This position is for some independent of, and for others dependent on, the will of God. As for those who think that the stars determine, independently of God's will, what we are to do and have and suffer, they should be given no hearing by anyone. . . .

For the moment, my argument is not directed against sincere pagans, but only against those who, in defense of what they call gods, attack the Christian religion. However, even those who think the stars are dependent on the will of God (in determining what human beings are to be and have and suffer) do the heavens a great wrong, if they image that the stars have their power so communicated to them by God's supreme power that they remain responsible for what they determine. For, how can we suppose— if I may so speak—that the unblemished justice of that brilliant Senate of the Stars could choose to have crimes committed, the like of which no state on earth could command without facing a sentence of suppression at the bar of world opinion?

God is the Lord of both stars and men. But, what kind of rule over men's actions is left to God if men are necessarily determined by the stars? (*City of God* 5.1)

When Augustine moves to a positive statement of providence, he is beautiful and lyrical. The reader must recall that St. Augustine was still the supreme theologian in the Western church at the time of St. Francis. The saint of Assisi grew up in an Augustinian world, and the sermons he heard were most often taken from the works of Augustine or his disciples. In the following passages, I think we hear the ideas that eight hundred years later would be woven by Francis into his mystical experience and recorded in "The Canticle of Brother Sun."

This supreme and true God—with His Word and Holy Spirit which are one with Him—this one omnipotent God is the creator and maker of every soul and of every body. All who find their joy in truth and not in mere shadows derive their happiness from Him. He made man a rational animal, composed of soul and body. He permitted man to sin—but not with impunity—and He pursued him with His mercy. He gave men—both good and bad—their being, as He gave being to the rocks. He let men share generative life in common with the trees, and the life of the senses with the beasts of the fields, but the life of intelligence only with the angels. God is the Author of all measure, form and order; of all size, number and weight. He is the source of every nature, of whatever sort or condition; of the seed of every form and the form of every seed and the movement of both seeds and forms. He gave to all flesh its beginning, beauty, health, and power of reproduction; the arrangement of its members and the general well-being of a balanced whole. To His irrational creatures He gave memory, perception, and appetite, but to His rational creatures He added a mind with intelligence and will.

He left no part of his creation without its appropriate peace, for in the last and least of all His living things the very entrails are wonderfully ordered—not to mention the beauty of birds' wings, and the flowers of the fields and the leaves of trees. And above the beauty of sky and earth is that of angels and of man. How, then, can anyone believe that it was the will of God to exempt from the laws of His providence the rise and fall of political societies? (*City of God* 5.11)

The Will Is All-Important

We cannot understand Augustine, or even the Gospels, unless we comprehend the crucial importance of the human will in the drama of salvation. It is often said that the modern world does not accept the idea of sin. I believe that this is only secondary. The real problem is that we do not appreciate the significance of the human will and its desire. Augustine makes this clear.

Man's will, then, is all-important. If it is badly directed, the emotions will be perverse; if it is rightly directed, the emotions will be not merely blameless but even praiseworthy. The will is in all of these affections; indeed, they are nothing else but inclinations of the will. For, what are desire and joy but the will in harmony with things we desire? And what are fear and sadness but the will in disagreement with things we abhor?

The consent of the will in the search for what we want is called desire; joy is the name of the will's consent to the enjoyment of what we desire. So, too, fear is aversion from what we do not wish to happen, as sadness is a disagreement of the will with something that happened against our will. Thus, according as the will of a man is attracted or repelled by the variety of things which he either seeks or shuns, so is it changed or converted into one or other of these different emotions.

It is clear, then, that the man who does not live according to man but according to God must be a lover of the good and, therefore, a hater of evil; since no man is wicked by nature but is wicked only by some defect, a man who lives according to God owes it to wicked men that his hatred be perfect, so that, neither hating the man because of his corruption nor loving the corruption because of the man, he should hate the sin but love the sinner. For, once the corruption has been cured, then all that is left should be loved and nothing remains to be hated. (*City of God* 14.6)

Angels and Human Beings Choose Happiness or Misery— The Origin of the Two Cities

The great drama of salvation begins not with the first parents but with those rational creatures who preceded them. Thus the stage is set not in the world of human beings but in the world of angels. It is very important to appreciate this fact if one is to understand the two different destinies of angels and human beings, beatitude or damnation. This distinction is the origin of the two cities—the good souls, angels and human beings desiring God, and the bad, who are losing him. In an age when the need to seek for salvation is so lightly dismissed and even the possibility of eternal loss is denied, it can be very salutary to recall the profound reasons for this basic Christian dogma, which echoes the warning of Christ in his admonitions and in his parables.

There is no reason to doubt that the contrary dispositions which have developed among these good and bad angels are due, not to different natures and origins, for God the Author and Creator of all substances has created them both, but to the dissimilar choices and desires of these angels themselves. Some, remaining faithful to God, the common good of all, have lived in the enjoyment of His eternity, truth, and love, while others, preferring the enjoyment of their own power, as though they were their own good, departed from the higher good and common blessedness for all and turned to goods of their own choosing.

Preferring the pomp of pride to this sublimity of eternity, the craftiness of vanity to the certainty of truth, and the turmoil of dissension to the union of love, they became proud, deceitful and envious.

Since the happiness of all angels consists in union with God, it follows that their unhappiness must be found in the very contrary, that is, in not adhering to God. To the question: "Why are the good angels happy?" the right answer is: "Because they adhere to God." To the question: "Why are the others unhappy?" the answer is: "Because they do not adhere to God." In fact, there is no other good which can make any rational or intellectual creature happy except God. Not every creature has the potentialities for happiness. Beasts, trees, stones, and such things neither acquire nor have the capacity for this gift. However, every creature which has this capacity receives it, not from itself, since it has been created out of nothing, but from its Creator. To possess Him is to be happy; to lose Him is to be in misery. And, of course, that One whose beatitude depends upon Himself as His own good and not on any other good can never be unhappy since He can never lose Himself. Thus, there can be no unchangeable good except our one, true, and blessed God. (*City of God* 12.1)

The history of human beings in their journey toward the possession of God is quite different from that of the angels. Because of the nature of their being angels had but one choice to make. Human beings, because of their limitations and the mercy of God, were not only given many choices, but they were redeemed by an awesome price.

In considering the salvation history of the human race, Augustine takes up the narrative of creation and the fall of the first human being. He discusses many aspects of this mysterious beginning as he does in his great work *The Literal Meaning of Genesis*.[3] He especially discusses the nature of death—that is, death as we know it, an experience of sorrow and loss rather than a joyful experience of going home to God. But overshadowing all of these issues, St. Augustine rejoices in the salvation bought only by the eternal Son of God, a grace of redemption absolutely necessary for any human being to come to the final goal of life, union with God. Augustine not only rejoices in salvation but insists that by the grace of the Savior the evil effects of the fall of the human race give rise to greater victories. Thus even *death* becomes, in the case of a martyr, a sign not of the fall but of the redemption.

This was apparently an important point to make because some had raised the question, logical enough if farfetched, "Why do those who are baptized still suffer the death of the body since this death was one of the effects of original sin?" Augustine's answer is that if the baptized did not die everyone would run to receive the sacrament. But since grace transforms death into a victory beyond the world of senses, the death of martyrs remains a victory of faith, because a victory unseen.

In former ages, at least, there was need to face the fear of death with a robust and aggressive faith, as was so clear in the case of the holy martyrs. Indeed, these saints would have enjoyed no glory and no victory, since there could have been no strife, if, once they were made holy by the waters of regeneration, they could suffer no bodily death. Who would not run to join the infants about to be baptized, if the main purpose of Christ's grace were to save us from bodily death? Thus, faith would be put to no test by an invisible reward; it could not even be called faith; it would be merely a desire to receive an immediate reward of its work. But now, by a greater and more wonderful grace of the Saviour, the punishment of sin serves the purposes of sanctity. In the beginning, the first man was warned: "If you sin, you shall die"; now, the martyr is admonished; "Die that you may not sin." The first man was told: "If you transgress, you shall die the death"; now, the martyr is reminded: "If you refuse death, you transgress the commandment." What before was to be feared, if a man were to keep himself from sin, is now to be faced, if he is not to sin. Thus, by the ineffable mercy of God, the penalty of sin is transformed into the panoply of virtue and the punishment of the sinner into the testing of a saint.

This does not mean that death, which before was an evil, has now become something good. But it means that God has rewarded faith with so much grace that death, which seems to be the enemy of life, becomes an ally that helps man enter into life. (*City of God* 13.4)

The Possibility of Establishing the City of God on Earth

It would appear from Western European history that several attempts have been made to establish a Christian society on the general outline of *City of God.* Sometimes these attempts have been almost bombastically explicit like the Holy Roman Empire or the reigns of the Catholic kings, who were even given the designation "apostolic" because they appointed bishops and provided for the spreading of the gospel in non-Christian lands. The history of Protestantism is replete with similar attempts (like the establishment of the Pilgrim enclave in Massachusetts or the Zionism of the Mormons), although these make no explicit reference to St. Augustine. In the rhetoric of the American political forum one even hears echoes, often naïve and manipulative, of the attempt to establish the perfect society with freedom and justice for all. The serious reader of *City of God* cannot come away with the idea that Augustine ever expected the establishment of the city of God here on earth, although he hoped for a state where sinners struggling to be disciples would set up a better world community than those that had previously been known. I think it would be safe to say that Augustine would expect that the more people who turned their desires to God and the service of God, the more likely a better society for all would come to pass. Augustine was quite explicit that the Christian following *City of God* had to work for a better social life for all. Referring to the pagan philosophers Augustine wrote:

What we Christians like better is their teaching that the life of virtue should be a social life. For, if the life of the saints had not been social, how could the City of God (which we have been discussing in all these nineteen Books) have a beginning, make progress, and reach its appointed goal? Yet, social living, given the misery of our mortality, has enormous drawbacks—more than can be easily counted, or known for what they really are. . . . . All human relationships are fraught with such misunderstandings. Not even the pure-hearted affection of friends is free from them.

All history is a tale of "slights and fights and spirits vexed," and we must expect such unpleasantness as an assured thing, whereas peace is a good unguaranteed—dependent upon the unknowable interior dispositions of our friends. Even if we could read their hearts today, anything might happen tomorrow. Take the members of a single family, who are as fond of one another as, in general, they are or, at least, are expected to be? Yet, who can rely utterly even on family affection? How much unhappiness has sprung from the ambush of domestic disloyalties! And how galling the disillusionment after peace had been so sweet—or seemed to be, though in fact it was nothing but a clever counterfeit. That is why no one can read, without a sigh, those touching words of Cicero: "No snares are ever so insidious as those lurking as dutiful devotion or labeled as family affection. You can easily escape from an open foe, but when hatred lurks in the bosom of a family it has taken a position and has pounced upon you before it can be spied out or recognized for what it is."

Even divine Revelation reminds us: "And a man's enemies will be those of his own household." It breaks the heart of any good man to hear this, for, even if he be brave enough to bear, or vigilant enough to beware of, the ruses of faithless friends, he must suffer greatly just the same when he discovers how treacherous they are. And it makes no difference whether they were genuine friends who have turned traitors, or traitorous men who had been trading on pretended affection all along.

If, then, the home, every man's haven in the storms of life, affords no solid security, what shall one say of the civic community? The bigger a city is, the fuller it is of legal battles, civil and criminal, and the more frequent are wild and bloody seditions or civil wars. Even when the frays are over, there is never any freedom from fear. (*City of God* 19.5)

For this and many other passages it can be seen that Augustine was no utopian. He hoped for a world community, but he realized that the ultimate community was the community of love that would come to pass only in eternity.

The Just War?

Since there is so much ink spilled on Augustine's idea of a just war, the reader might care to read exactly what he had to say, which is quite different from what he is usually quoted as having said:

After the city comes the world community. This is the third stage in the hierarchy of human associations. First, we have the home; then the city; finally, the globe. And, of course, as with the perils of the ocean, the bigger the community, the fuller it is of misfortunes. The first misfortune is the lack of communication resulting from language differences. It will be answered that the Roman Empire, in the interests of peaceful collaboration, imposes on nations it has conquered the yoke of both law and language, and thus has an adequate, or even an overflowing, abundance of interpreters. True enough. But at what cost! There is one war after another, havoc everywhere, tremendous slaughterings of men.

All this for peace. Yet, when the wars are waged, there are new calamities brewing. To begin with, there never has been, nor is there today, any absence of hostile foreign powers to provoke war. What is worse, the very development of the empire accruing from their incorporation has begotten still worse wars within. I refer to the civil wars and social uprisings that involve even more wretched anxieties for human beings, either shaken by their actual impact, or living in fear of their renewal. Massacres, frequent and sweeping, hardships too dire to endure are but a part of the ravages of war. I am utterly unable to describe them as they are, and as they ought to be described; and even if I should try to begin, where could I end?

I know the objection that a good ruler will wage wars only if they are just. But, surely, if he will only remember that he is a man, he will begin by bewailing the necessity he is under of waging even just wars. A good man would be under compulsion to wage no wars at all, if there were not such things as just wars. A just war, moreover, is justified only by the injustice of an aggressor; and that injustice ought to be a source of grief to any good man, because it is human injustice. It would be deplorable in itself, apart from being a source of conflict. (*City of God* 19.7)

Some have thought that the city of God may refer to the visible church on earth. Certainly these people were not familiar with Augustine's thought or even the context of this great work. Augustine had no illusions about the church or even those who had been assigned as its shepherds. In his *Sermons* to priests and bishops he often calls for repentance and true discipleship and made no secret about those who fail in their office as servants of the gospel and of the people of God.

The following quotation from a sermon on the occasion of the ordination of the bishop in Carthage in 411 shows that the great bishop himself lacked neither realism nor wit when it came to the foibles of the clergy.

That is the sort of person a good bishop ought to be; otherwise, he is no bishop. What use is it to an unfortunate man to have the name Lucky? If you saw a miserable beggar whose name was Lucky and addressed him by his name, saying "Come here Lucky; go there, Lucky; get up, Lucky; sit down, Lucky—then, despite his name, he would continue to be unfortunate. Something similar happens when you address a man as bishop who is not a bishop at heart. What does the honor of the name bring him, except a heap of reproach?

But who is the bishop who is called a bishop and is not one? He who rejoices in that honor rather than the salvation of God's flock, who in that high office seeks his own ends, not those of Jesus Christ. He is called a bishop but is not a bishop; the name is of no use to him, but no one calls him anything else. Have you seen the bishop? Have you greeted the bishop?, they ask.

Therefore, to be worthy of his name, let him listen not to me but with me—let us listen together, and as fellow pupils in one school let us learn together from the one master, Christ, whose chair is in heaven, because it was first the cross on earth. He has taught us the way of humility, descending to ascend, visiting those who lie in the lowest depths, and raising those who wanted to be united to him. (*Sermon* 340A)[4]

Such sharply realistic observations must be balanced by a recognition of Augustine's love for the church and its worship and offices. He saw the church as the family of disciples, served and governed at the same time by the bishops, offering to God the worship of repentance and continuous conversion.

Both in outward signs and inner devotion, we owe to Him that service which the Greeks call *latreia*. Indeed, all of us together, and each one in particular, constitute His temple because He deigns to take for a dwelling both the community of all and the person of each individual. Nor is He greater in all than in each, since He cannot be extended by numbers nor diminished by being shared. When raised to Him, our heart becomes His altar;

His only Son is the priest who wins for us His favor. It is only by the shedding of our blood in fighting for His truth that we offer Him bloody victims. We burn the sweetest incense in His sight when we are aflame with holy piety and love. As the best gifts we consecrate and surrender to Him our very selves which He has given us. We dedicate and consecrate to Him the memory of His bounties by establishing appointed days as solemn feasts, lest, by the lapse of time, ingratitude and forgetfulness should steal upon us. On the altar of our heart, we offer to Him a sacrifice of humility and praise, aglow with the fire of charity.

It is this Good which we are commanded to love with our whole heart, with our whole mind, and with all our strength. It is toward this Good that we should be led by those who love us, and toward this Good we should lead those whom we love. In this way, we fulfill the commandments on which depend the whole Law and the Prophets. . . .

This, then, is the worship of God; this is true religion and the right kind of piety; this is the service that is due only to God. (*City of God* 10.3)

The Two Cities Coexist

Saint Augustine lists many qualities of the citizens of the city of God. He says that in the earthly city temple goods are used for the enjoyment of earthly power, whereas in the heavenly city they are used with a view of the enjoyment of eternal peace.[5] The citizen of the heavenly city lives by faith as a pilgrim and refers all peace of body and soul to the higher peace which unites a mortal man with the immortal God.[6] The city of God has no concern for dress or manners of the person of faith so long as these do not offend the divine law: "For it is faith and not fashions that bring us to God."[7] The citizen may pursue the active or contemplative or contemplative–active life so long as he loves truth and does what charity demands.[8]

When it comes to the ultimate goal of life, the two cities are very different. Here he presents the earthly city at its natural best. You will recall he spoke well of the early days of the Roman Republic because at that time natural virtues flourished.

So, too, the earthly city which does not live by faith seeks only an earthly peace, and limits the goal of its peace, of its harmony of authority and obedience among its citizens, to the voluntary and collective attainment of objectives necessary to mortal existence. The heavenly city, meanwhile—or, rather, that part that is on pilgrimage in mortal life and lives by faith—must use this earthly peace until such time as our mortality which needs such peace has passed away. As a consequence, so long as her life in the earthly city is that of a captive and an alien (although she has the promise of ultimate delivery and the gift of the Spirit as a pledge), she has no hesitation about keeping in step with the civil law which governs matters pertaining to our existence here below. For, as moral life is the same for all, there ought to be common cause between the two cities in what concerns our purely human living. (*City of God* 19.17)

The citizens of the two cities can and must cooperate in the welfare of the human community and in the struggle for peace in the world. This is not the invisible community of love that Augustine speaks of in *City of God* but rather a makeshift arrangement, which is, after all, the best we can hope for in this fallen world.

So long, then, as the heavenly City is wayfaring on earth, she invites citizens from all nations and all tongues, and unites them into a single pilgrim band. She takes no issue with that diversity of customs, laws, and traditions whereby human peace is sought and maintained. Instead of nullifying or tearing down, she preserves and appropriates whatever in the diversities of divers races is aimed at one and the same objective of human peace, provided only that they do not stand in the way of the faith and worship of the one supreme and true God.

Thus, the heavenly City, so long as it is wayfaring on earth, not only makes use of earthly peace but fosters and actively pursues along with other human beings a common platform in regard to all that concerns our purely human life and does not interfere with faith and worship. Of course, though, the City of God subordinates this earthly peace to that of heaven. For this is not merely true peace, but strictly speaking, for any rational creature, the only real peace, since it is, as I said, "the perfectly ordered and harmonious communion of those who find their joy in God and in one another in God." (*City of God* 19.17)

What Peace Do We Have Here?

The peace of heaven is promised to the citizens of the city of God, but what peace do they experience now? It is certainly not the peace of eternity. In order to avoid confusion about the good life on earth and eternal life, Augustine suggests that we distinguish between "peace in this life" and "peace in the next." The latter peace is our highest good.[9] Our peace on earth is at best problematic.

Not even the holy and faithful followers of the one true and supreme God are beyond the reach of demonic trickery and temptation in its many forms. Yet our anxiety in this matter is good for us, so long as we inhabit this frail body in this evil world, for it sends us seeking more ardently after that heavenly peace which is to be unshakable and unending. There, all of our natural endowments—all that the Creator of all natures has given to our nature—will be both good and everlasting, where every wound in the soul is to be healed by wisdom and every weakness of body to be removed by resurrection; where our virtues will be no longer at war with passion or opposition of any kind, but are to have, as the prize of victory, an eternally imperturbable peace. This is what is meant by that consummate beatitude, that limitless perfection, that end that never ends.

On earth we are happy, after a fashion, when we enjoy the peace, little as it is, which a good life brings; but such happiness compared with the beatitude which is our end in eternity is, in point of fact, misery. When we mortal men, living amid the realities of earth, enjoy the utmost peace which life can give us, then it is the part of virtue, if we are living rightly, to make a right use of the goods we are enjoying. When, on the other hand, we do not enjoy this temporal peace, then it is the function of virtue to make a right use of the misfortunes which we are suffering. (*City of God* 19.10)

The Christians must keep their eyes on eternity—their true home. The peace they seek is a peace that the world cannot give. In these days one may find such a teaching jarring. It does not go along with the general Dr. Feelgood notions of this superficial age—but it is most unlikely that these notions will survive for a long time. In some quarters, Augustine is accused of pessimism, but when one's goal is clearly eternal life and its everlasting peace, one can only be called a pessimist in limited ways.

He is disconcertingly realistic even in the peace we have from the hope of eternal life. This, he calls, "peace of faith." Its strongest and most powerful expression for Augustine is not some triumph song but the prayer of repentance so that we may rely on God. His final days were spent in meditating on the words, "Create in me a clean heart, O God" and "My sin is ever before me."[10] He sums up the peace of faith in this way:

The City of God, however, has a peace of its own, namely, peace with God in this world by faith and in the world to come by vision. Still, any peace we have on earth, whether the peace we share with Babylon or our own peace through faith, is more like a solace for unhappiness than the joy of beatitude. Even our virtue in this life, genuine as it is because it is referred to the true goal of every good, lies more in the pardoning of sins than in any perfection of virtues. Witness the prayer of God's whole City, wandering on earth and calling out to Him through all her members: "Forgive us our debts as we also forgive our debtors." (*City of God* 19.27)

Augustine never lets the citizens of the city of God get away with presumption. He is not one to tell people that they are saved irrevocably; he could hardly be the student of St. Paul that he was and make such a mistake.

Who, then, save a proud man, will presume that he can live without needing to ask God: "Forgive us our debts"? Not a great man, you may be sure, but one blown up with the wind of self-reliance—one whom God in His justice resists while He grants His grace to the humble. Hence, it is written: "God resists the proud, but gives grace to the humble."

This, then, in this world, is the life of virtue. When God commands, man obeys; when the soul commands, the body obeys; when reason rules, our passions, even when they fight back, must be conquered or resisted; man must beg God's grace to win merit and the remission of his sins and must thank God for the blessings he receives. (*City of God* 19.27)

What Awaits the City of God
and the Earthly City?

Augustine has a long description in book 20 of the last judgment based on biblical texts and the interpretation of his times. He very literally states that Christ will come from heaven to judge the living and the dead. He speaks of reward and punishment, although in total consistency with his whole teaching he qualifies reward by saying that "no good action can be done without divine help" (*City of God* 20.1). He does not stand back from outlining the judgment of the wicked although he says that God may "be more sparing to one and more severe with another according to the individual's wickedness" (*City of God* 20.1).

It may be well for us in these significant times to meditate on the following passage:

But, in that final peace which is the end and purpose of all virtue here on earth, our nature, made whole by immortality and incorruption, will have no vices and experience no rebellion from within or without. There will be no need for reason to govern non-existent evil inclinations. God will hold sway over man, the soul over the body; and the happiness in eternal life and law will make obedience sweet and easy. And in each and all of us this condition will be everlasting, and we shall know it to be so. That is why the peace of such blessedness or the blessedness of such peace is to be our supreme good.

On the other hand, the doom in store for those who are not of the City of God is an unending wretchedness that is called "the second death," because neither the soul, cut off from the life of God, nor the body, pounded by perpetual pain, can there be said to live at all. And what will make that second death so hard to bear is that there will be no death to end it. (*City of God* 19.27)

The Center of the Drama of the Two Cities

The climax of this entire drama of the two cities is not the last judgment. That is its denouement or conclusion. The central fact is the passion, death, and resurrection of the Mediator between God and the human race, Jesus Christ.

The mediation of Christ, the Savior, and the doctrine of the Mystical Body have been already reviewed above in chapter 4. However, any consideration of *City of God* would be meaningless unless this central fact, the saving sacrifice of Christ, is seen as the center of the drama. There is no city of God without this. We let Augustine speak for himself.

Christ Jesus, Himself man, is the true Mediator, for, inasmuch as He took the "form of a slave," He became the "Mediator between God and men." In His character as God, He receives sacrifices in union with the Father, with whom He is one God; yet He chose, in His character as a slave, to be Himself the Sacrifice rather than to receive it, lest any one might take occasion to think that sacrifice could be rendered to a creature. Thus it is that He is both the Priest who offers and the Oblation that is offered. And it was His will that as a sacrament of this reality there should be the daily sacrifice of the Church, which, being the Body of Him, her Head, learns to offer itself through Him. This is the true sacrifice of which the ancient sacrifices of the saints were but many and manifold symbols. This one sacrifice was prefigured, in a variety of ways, as though one idea were being expressed in many words to drive in the truth without boring the reader. It is the supreme and true sacrifice to which all false sacrifices have given place. (*City of God* 10.20)

From the review of this great work, it is obvious that *City of God* contains much more than the defense of the Christian faith against the Roman pagans. It is a gold mine of theology so presented that apparently dry ideas come to life to enlighten and inflame the devout reader. This great work can help any serious reader to grow in the richness of faith and love. This is because the writer himself always did his work so that he himself might grow in loving faith.

✛ **Chapter Seven** ✛

Augustine as
a Spiritual Guide

High in the Alps, sometimes almost up to the highest extent of the trees, one finds little chapels. These are simple and beautiful—modestly expressing the human attempt to say something about God amidst the grandeur of his creation. Mountains have always been places where human beings attempted to meet God, and sometimes this has happened. In the Bible we find Mount Sinai, Mount Nebo, Mount Zion, Mount Tabor, Mount Calvary. Mount Calvary, although an ugly knob, was assigned this majestic title because of a feeling that somehow it had to be a mountain. Europe has its Mount Athos, Mount St. Michael, Monte Cassino, Monte Alverno, and Croagh Patrick to name only a few. All are crowned with chapels or even large places of worship. I have to put a little chapel, white and simple with a slender spire, here in my Augustinian Alps. This is where I will think about making a visit to someone who has been my spiritual guide for almost half a century. Although I have been reading and studying his works all that time, he always has something new to say to me. It is difficult for me to select a few topics so that you will have a taste of his teaching, but I shall try. Much of what we have looked at already is spiritual teaching and counsel of the highest sort.

Faith, Hope, and Charity

My meditation in an Alpine chapel brings up another vision of a modest religious house. Augustine always lived with his community of priests and brothers. The house is far from the Alps and is, in fact, in the hot climate of North Africa. If you and I had been able to visit Hippo around 420 and had been received by the bishop when he was an older man, after he had finished up much of his work, we probably would have asked him, "What is the essence of the Christian life?" He would have given us the simple answer, "The life of faith, hope, and charity." You might have been disappointed by this obvious response—it almost sounds like a banality. You might have responded, "So what's new?" and then he would proceed to tell us things about these virtues you might not even have thought about. He would no doubt ask you what everybody seeks and desires, and you would obviously say, "Happiness." Since you are a believer you know already that this happiness comes from God, at least any happiness that does not fade and die. How do we find that happiness and the eternal good whose presence is its cause? How can we find or catch up with God? The bishop would put this question to us. Then he would sit forward on his chair and ask some questions that he would answer himself:

How can we follow after Him whom we do not see? or how can we see Him, we who are not only men, but also men of weak under-standing? For though God is seen not with the eyes but with the mind, where can such a mind be found as shall, while obscured by foolishness, succeed or even attempt to drink in that light? We must therefore have recourse to the instructions of those whom we have reason to think wise. That is as far as rational argument goes. For in human things reasoning is employed, not as of greater certainty, but as easier from use. But when we come to divine things, this faculty turns away; it cannot behold; it pants and gasps and burns with desire; it falls back from the light of truth and turns again to its customary obscurity, not from choice but from exhaustion. What a dreadful catastrophe is this, that the soul should be reduced to greater helplessness when it is seek-ing rest. So, when we are hastening to retire into darkness, it will be well that by the appointment of adorable Wisdom we should be met by the friendly outreach of authority, and should be attracted by the wonderful character of its contents, and by the utterance of its pages which, like shadows, typify and gently lead us to the truth. What more could have been done for our salvation?

Let us see how the Lord Himself in the gospel has taught us to live; how, too, Paul the apostle. Let us hear, O Christ, what chief end he prescribes to us; and that is evidently the chief end after which we are told to strive with supreme affection. "You shall Love," He says, "the Lord your God." Tell me also, what must be the measure of love; for I fear lest the desire enkindled in my heart should either exceed or come short in fervor. "With all your heart," He says. Nor is that enough. "With all your soul." Nor is it enough yet. "With all your mind." What do you wish more? I might perhaps wish more if I could see the possibility of more. What does Paul say on this? "We know," he says, "that all things work together for the good of them that love God." Let him, too, say what is the measure of love. "Who then," he asks, "shall separate us from the love of Christ? shall tribulation or distress or persecution or famine or nakedness or peril or the sword?" We have heard, then, what and how much we must love; this we must strive after, and to this we must refer all out plans. The perfection of all our good things and our perfect good is God. We must neither come short of this nor go beyond it; the one is dangerous, the other impossible.[1]

After a response like this we would probably have sat there in stunned silence and recovered our wits enough to ask, "How does one continue to grow in faith, hope, and charity?" The bishop of Hippo would smile and say, "That's a coincidence—if there are such things. I think it's all providence myself. But I just happen to have written a little scroll on this very subject." He would take it down from the scroll rack and dust it off. "I wrote a letter on that very subject to a very fine spiritual woman named Proba. She had written asking, 'What about prayer?' That's a partial answer. You see, the daily offices and prayers of the church, the attendance at the liturgy, even just getting in morning and evening prayers, are important to remind us of who we are and where we are going in the spiritual life, but we must always pray for a pure heart. There is someone at the door. Why don't you glance over this letter while I see what it is. It's probably the Donatists with some gripe or another."

Why in our fear of not praying as we should, do we turn to so many things, to find what we should pray for? Why do we not say instead, in the words of the psalm: *I have asked one thing from the Lord, this is what I will seek: to dwell in the Lord's house all the days of my life to see the graciousness of the Lord, and to visit his temple.* There the days do not come and go in succession, and the beginning of one day does not mean the end of another; all days are one, simultaneously and without end, and the life lived out in these days has itself no end.

So that we might obtain this life of happiness, he who is true life itself taught us to pray, not in many words as though speaking longer could gain us a hearing. After all, we pray to one who, as the Lord Himself tells us, knows what we need before we ask for it.

Why He should ask us to pray, when He knows what we need before we ask Him, may perplex us if we do not realize that our Lord and God does not want to know what we want (for He cannot fail to know it) but wants us rather to exercise our desire through our prayers so that we may be able to receive what he is preparing to give us. His gift is very great indeed, but our capacity is too small and limited to receive it. That is why we are told: *Enlarge your desires, do not bear the yoke with unbelievers.*

The deeper our faith, the stronger our hope, the greater our desire, the larger will be our capacity to receive that gift, which is very great indeed. *No eye has seen it:* it has no color. *No ear has heard it;* it has no sound. *It has not entered man's heart;* man's heart must enter into it.

In this faith, hope and love we pray always with unwearied desire. However, at set times and seasons we also pray to God in words, so that by these signs we may instruct ourselves and mark the progress we have made in our desire, and spur ourselves on to deepen it. The more fervent the desire, the more worthy will be its fruit. When the Apostle tells us: *Pray without ceasing,* he means this: desire unceasingly that life of happiness which is nothing if not eternal and ask it of Him who alone is able to give it. (*Letter* 130)[2]

If we had the opportunity to read this passage and perhaps a bit more extensively in the letter, we could easily deduce some of the things necessary to grow in the life of the virtues. One is obviously prayer, which is discussed in this letter; another is desire, and in other places Augustine has stressed this; then there is love of neighbor and purity of heart. We will ask him about this when he returns.

He might say to us in response to your mentioning desire, "O yes, that has always been important to me. I've heard that they even call me a 'eudemonist,' among other things. That means I really believe all enjoyment in life should be directed toward finding God—and I do believe that—so long as the enjoyment is moral, properly balanced, and always relating to our salvation. I don't think that we should ever do anything in this life that does not contribute to our salvation or that of our neighbors. Someone called me a puritan and mean about some of the normal pleasures of life. They forget that I sadly had a lot of experience with pleasure before my conversion and most of it was not directed toward finding God. In fact, God forgive me, it was directed away from finding the real God. Like many people, I was busy making up a god who was fashioned after my own ideas."

He would then get a faraway look in his eyes and say something like, "I don't know why; I never understood it, but all those long years when I led a bad life and broke my poor mother's heart, I was literally haunted by a desire to know and love God, the eternal truth and the eternal beauty. Once I got onto the scent of God, so to speak, through reading the philosophers and the Scriptures (which I thought were very beautiful, but I did not know they were God's own words), I really burned with a desire to know and love him. But I ran into a wall until I went back to the faith I had lost, if I ever really had it, and I became completely entranced with Jesus—everything about him—what he said, what he did, what he prayed. But I did find out from Scripture that I could never see God or know God perfectly in this life but that sometimes I could get a glimpse of him and be lifted up on a high (I think that's what you say now), and sometimes I would come crashing down and walk the rough roads again. So that's the Christian life, an uphill struggle motivated by a desire for the God who is good, true, and beautiful—a desire that is sometimes partly satisfied. Most of the time, however, we are just pushed along the way by a burning desire that will be fulfilled only when we get to the kingdom of heaven, which is what we are really waiting for. Desire is then the key, a holy desire purified from selfishness and sensuality and constantly fed by God's grace. As I wrote to Proba, prayer expresses that desire, keeps it going."

Let us always desire the happy life from the Lord God and always pray for it. But for this very reason we turn our mind to the task of prayer at appointed hours, since that desire grows lukewarm, so to speak, from our involvement in other concerns and occupations. We remind ourselves through the words of prayer to focus our attention on the object of our desire, otherwise, the desire that began to grow lukewarm may grow chill altogether and may be totally extinguished unless it is repeatedly stirred into flame. (*Letter* 130)

You might ask then, "What is a pure or clean heart that can bring us closer to God? Does it mean chastity is a way to God?"

Augustine would answer that of course a pure heart means a chaste heart in all walks of life. He had written about chastity in the *Confessions* and in his books on virginity. Different kinds of chastity are for different ways of life, and certainly chastity was part of marriage. He mentioned that he had also written on marriage and been misunderstood. But he would answer our question, "A pure heart is not only a chaste heart but one that has an intention of always pleasing God, of doing everything consistently with its goal firmly fixed on God, guided by Scripture and by the church." More and more as one grows in the pursuit of God, which is seeking for God alone and doing all for him, you might ask how one can tell if one is doing this. And he might answer, "I preached a sermon (138) some time ago to bishops and priests on that very subject, because they must serve God with a pure heart if they are going to take the place of the Good Shepherd." He then quoted from his sermon. He began by quoting Matthew 7:21–23:

He (our Lord) says that some preach the gospel for love, others for opportunity, about whom he says, *They do not preach the gospel rightly.* The matter is right, but they themselves are wrong. What they preach is right, but the preachers are wrong. Why are they wrong? Because they seek something else in the Church; they are not seeking God. If they sought God, they would be chaste, for God is the soul's legitimate husband. Whoever seeks something from God other than God does not seek God chastely.

You see, my friends, if a wife loves her husband because he is wealthy, then she is not chaste, for rather than loving her husband, she loves his money. If she truly loves her husband, she will love him even when he is poor, even when he has nothing. But if she loves him because of his wealth, what happens if (such are the chances of human life) his property is confiscated and he suddenly finds himself destitute? Perhaps she will renounce him because what she loved was not her husband but his possessions. But if she truly loves her husband, she loves him even more as a poor man, for she loves with compassion.

And yet, my friends, our God can never be poor. He is rich, he has made all things, heaven and earth, the sea and the angels. Whatever we can see in the heavens and whatever is beyond our sight he has created. Even so, it is none of these treasures that we must love, but their creator, for all He has promised you is Himself. Find something more precious, and He will give it to you. The earth, the sky and the angels are glorious things but even more glorious is He who has created them. So those who preach God because they love God, those who preach God because of God, feed His sheep and are not hirelings. It was the chastity of the soul that our Lord Jesus Christ demanded when He asked Peter, *Peter, do you love me?* What does it mean, *Do you love me* (John 21:15)? Are you chaste? Have you a heart that is not adulterous? Do you seek in the Church, not your own interests, but mine? If, then, you are such a person and you love me, *feed my sheep.* You will not be a hireling but a shepherd. (*Sermon* 138)[3]

As the bishop stopped reading he would glance out the window of his office toward the cathedral church, which was very unpretentious. He might then have said, "But we cannot do this without Christ. I have often tried to preach what our Savior meant when he said, 'I am the vine, you are the branches.' The heart of the members and the body of Christ become pure by

God's grace through Him who is the Head of the body; that is, through Jesus Christ, our Lord. The cleansing of our rebirth! I have often said in my sermons on the psalms that we not only pray to him, but with him. He is the one that prays in our midst."

Then the bishop might start to get emphatic with us. He would say that, as pious as all of this sounds, it is just one long lie (a favorite expression of his) if we don't love and serve our neighbor. He would get another scroll out and sit down with an intense look and read from *Sermon* 90, which is about the necessity of wearing the wedding garment of charity to be admitted to the banquet of God.

So extend your love, and not only as far as your husbands, wives and children. That degree of love is to be found even among cattle and sparrows. You know how these sparrows and swallows love their mates; they share the task of sitting on the eggs, together they feed their chicks, out of a charming and natural goodness, without a thought for any reward. I mean the sparrow husband doesn't say, "I will feed my children, so that when I grow old they may feed me." No such thoughts as that; he loves them freely, feeds them freely for nothing; he shows the affection of a parent, he doesn't expect any reward. You too, I know, I'm sure, love your children in the same way.

But extend your love, let this love grow, because loving children, husbands and wives is not yet that wedding garment. Have faith in God, trust him. First love God. Extend yourselves toward God, and grab whom you can for God. An enemy, perhaps; have him snatched for God. A son, a wife, a slave, have them snatched off to God. A stranger perhaps; have him snatched off to God. Grab, grab your enemy; by being grabbed he will cease to be an enemy.

That's the way we should be making progress: that's the way charity should be nourished, and eventually brought to perfection. That's how the wedding garment should be put on. That's how the image of God to which we were created should be progressively sculpted afresh. (*Sermon* 90)[4]

Then he would remind us what he had written in his book on the Trinity (which thankfully we are familiar with and could smile back with a look of honest recognition). He had written, "We find many other cases in the sacred writings where only love of neighbor seems to be required of us for perfection and the love of God seems to be passed over in silence, though the law and the prophets depend on both commandments. But this is because if a man loves his neighbor, it follows that above all he loves love itself. But *God is love and whoever abides in love abides in God* (1 Jn 4:16). So it follows that above all he loves God" (*The Trinity* 8.10; trans. Hill).

By this time there would be a line of people waiting to see him. He was very well known for helping all sorts of people—even his enemies. Despite his very strong conviction on the church as the Mystical Body of Christ, he had friends among the Donatists, the Jews, and even the sincere pagans.[5] You might say for those times he was a bit ecumenical.

As we begin to leave he would give us a piece of advice, "If you want to grow in the Christian life and purify the image of the holy Trinity that is already in your soul, you must love your brothers and sisters in Christ. You have to love and even enjoy and encourage the community. Being a good Christian is not just doing charitable deeds, it is encouraging everyone in the Christian community. Frequently, Christians encourage the fervor of others and add to their own." As he spoke of such encouragement, he picked up the scroll of the *Sermons on the Psalms*, which he had given to the newly baptized Christians. He spoke about enjoying a pilgrimage as a smile broke over his face. He read from the following passage:

"I rejoiced with this word which was spoken to me: We shall go into the house of the Lord" (Ps. 121:1). My Beloved, recall to mind that when one speaks on a feast of martyrs or at a holy shrine, a crowd assembles to celebrate the anniversary. These crowds mutually encourage one another, exhorting one another, saying: Let us go, let us go! And where shall we go, some say. To such a place, answer the others, to the consecrated shrine. They stimulate one another, are enkindled until little by little they form only one flame, and the unique flame, enkindled by each one's ardent words, carries them to the designated holy place while holy thought sanctifies them.

If then holy love thus urges them to a temporal place, what must be the love which hurries people with one heart and soul toward heaven, saying to one another: "Let us go into the house of the Lord"? Let us run, then, to go into the house of the Lord. Let us run, and not grow weary, for we shall arrive there where there is no more weariness.[6]

And as we move toward the door where the other people are waiting, he politely lets you know that he had something else to say. He would let us know that there was one thing missing—and he would not let us out. With a smile on his face he would motion us to sit down again with a quiet dramatic gesture—he was not beyond a touch of drama from his old days as a teacher of rhetoric. He would ask if you knew what three things are most important in the spiritual life. You might look blank for a moment, and then he would tell you. "Humility, humility, and then humility. I wrote something on humility in those sermons I just quoted to you. This is about Psalm 122 and what someone should do to avoid pride."

Let him lift up his eyes to Him who dwells in heaven, let him not heed himself. For every proud man heeds himself, and he who pleases himself seems great to himself. But he who pleases himself pleases a fool, for he himself is a fool when he is pleasing to himself. Only he who is pleasing to God is pleasing without danger. And who is pleasing to God? He whom God has pleased. God cannot displease Himself; may He please you also that you may be pleasing to Him. But unless you displease yourself, He cannot please you. But if you displease yourself, lift your eyes from yourself. Why do you have self-regard? For if you sincerely regard yourself, you find in yourself that which will displease you. And you say to God, "My sin is ever before me" (Ps. 51:3). Let your sin be before you that it may not be before God.[7]

Then, rising, he would accompany us to the door, continuing to speak, "You know," he would say, "we were saved by humility—the humility of God. The life of Christ is a life of humiliation and humility. The humiliation comes from us, but the humble acceptance of this humiliation was from God. Everybody knows I used to be a great sinner. I am still a sinner. I tell the faithful that

I am a sinner, and without the grace of Christ I would fall back in a minute to what I had then or worse. I have always said to God, "Command me to do what you want and give me the grace to obey your commands" (*Conf.* 10.29). "I make no secret that I still struggle with temptations, and I still get annoyed at this. I have to watch that I don't eat or drink too much (*Conf.* 10.31). We must look forward to being united with God, where there will be no more sorrow or toil, where we will live a real life, a full life, where we will be completely filled with God, not this half-life (*Conf.* 10.28). Then we will be happy. But who can understand it all? Can any man tell us? No. Can any angel tell us? No."

Then pausing to look up as if giving a blessing he would say: "Of You O Lord, we must ask, in You we must seek, at You we must knock. Only in this way shall we receive, only in this way shall we find, only in this way will it be opened to us" (*Conf.* 13.38).

An Apology

If you are a scholar (I don't think that many scholars will read this simple book for beginners) and if you should read this I ask that you would indulge me for using this form, quoting Augustine in substance and at times in his own words. It seemed to me that it would be an effective way of introducing him as a spiritual director. I have been a spiritual director myself, and I have been asked, "Who directs the spiritual directors while the spiritual directors direct the spirits?" Oftentimes, especially when one is old, it is difficult to find a director to take on the job. I have always had a director I could easily go to. I could read his words, ponder them, and argue with him sometimes. We know from his book of retractions that he was quite capable of changing his mind. I like to believe that I could speak to him, let him know my mind, ask his prayers, and those of his mother.

Augustine—His Own Summary

Long ago in a marvelous book called the *Augustine Synthesis*, I came across a section of a sermon obviously preached to convince the people of Hippo that they could not come to a firm belief in the Trinity unless they accepted the mystery of the cross of Christ. I memorized most of this text, and I have often quoted it. As I draw this introductory book to a close and, having surveyed with you the Augustinian Alps, I realize that this sermon is a summary of the great insights of St. Augustine. I am taking the liberty of including my own translation, in which I attempt to highlight the following teachings: the Trinity and how we come to it—by faith; that Christ our Redeemer is the single way to this knowledge and faith; that the cross is the key to understanding Christ; that the belief in him is in many ways linked to his divine signs when he lived on earth and to the many miracles worked in his name after the resurrection; that the world came to accept him without really understanding his humility; and that it is the humility of God that establishes the beginning of the city of God in history. This humility protects us from the greatest spiritual enemy we have—pride. Thus the *Confessions, The Trinity, The City of God,* and all of his teachings about total dependency on Christ and following Christ are all brought together in this single statement in *Letter* 232.[8]

The Confession of the Trinity

There is the Invisible Creator, origin and cause of all we see, from whom all being comes; He is supreme, eternal, unchanging and comprehended only by Himself. There is One by whom this supreme Ruler reveals Himself—The Word equal to Him by whom He is begotten and made known. There is One who is Holiness itself who makes holy all that is sanctified. He is the inseparable and undivided communion between the unchanging Word and that First Cause and Creator who proclaims Himself by this Word. And they are all equal to each other.

Who Can Know This?

Who can contemplate with calm and pure mind this whole being . . . and blessed by this contemplation press on to the sight of that which is beyond all known by our perception—to be clothed with everlasting life and obtain eternal salvation? Who can do this but someone who has admitted his sins, leveled his pride to the dust and knelt in meekness to receive God as his teacher?

But How?

This can only happen by getting rid of pride by humility of spirit so that we can be lifted up. Such a humility was provided for us in a way that was filled with glory but most gentle, converting our haughty hearts by persuasion rather than by force. This was done by the Word by whom God the Father reveals Himself to angels, His Son who is his Power and Wisdom, hidden from human hearts blinded by worldly desires, humbling Himself to come in human form. This humble example of God makes us more afraid of being proud than of being humiliated like Him.

The Christ Who Is Preached

Therefore, the Christ who is preached throughout the world is not wearing an earthly crown, nor a rich Christ, but Christ crucified. At first this Christ was ridiculed by many, and the ridicule goes on. A few believed at first but now whole nations. Because when Christ, despite the ridicule of men, was first preached the lame walked, the dumb spoke, the deaf heard and even the dead came back to life. This finally convinced some of the proud that even among the visible forces of the physical world there is nothing more powerful than the Humility of God. All this took place that we might struggle to be humble, shielded from the contemptible assaults of human pride by the example of a humble God.

Addenda

There are a few issues which really do not fit into this introductory volume but are so important for a complete picture of Augustine that I am putting them at the end as addenda. One is Augustine's immense contribution to religious life and his authorship of a great rule. The other is his attitude toward women. At the end of the addenda is a step-by-step reading program. But be careful! If you start reading you may never get out of the Augustinian Alps.

Augustine, the Religious

If we use the word "monk" just a bit loosely (as was done in the past at times and is still done so today) St. Augustine was a monk. He first started a community of laymen who were monks, then expanded it to priests who served the faithful of the diocese of Hippo. The term "monk" simply means a single person (*monos*) who lives in community and serves the Lord by prayers and good works. The disciplines or vows of religious life are poverty, chaste celibacy, and obedience. The great monastic movement of the West had yet to be launched by St. Benedict, and St. Basil's equally great monastic movement in the East was just taking hold. These movements would give a more cloistered meaning to the word "monk." Augustine's monks could be very much at home in the town or even the city. They would work either as priests in pastoral work or as lay Christians doing good works in the name of Christ. They were also given to a life of prayer and contemplation. They strove to lead a life of action mixed with prayer, which was called a mixed life in the time of St. Augustine.

The brief *Rule* that St. Augustine wrote is beautifully translated from a very authentic source by Sr. Clark and can be found at the end of *Augustine of Hippo.* Everyone interested in Augustine should read it. It is succinct, very down to earth, and no nonsense. It is not as long or as inspiring as the *Rule of St. Benedict* and is even shorter than the *Rule of St. Francis.* Because of its trim and practical content, Augustine's rule for men and the slightly adapted one for women have become foundations of religious life, especially for religious who strive to lead a life that is a mixture of prayerful contemplation and active ministry. For this reason this rule was adopted by hermits, by single religious or people living in very small communities in relative solitude, and by the canons of cathedrals and large churches where they banded together to pray and do pastoral work. When the canons followed the *Rule of St. Augustine* they were called "canons regular"; the adjective "regular" refers to the *Rule of St. Augustine.* For instance, St. Bernard of Menton (d.1008), whose canons worked to help Alpine travelers and after whom the great dog has been named, and St. Norbert, archbishop of Magdeburg (d.1134), who began the pastoral canons regular, followed the *Rule of St. Augustine.*

It may be said that St. Norbert really opened the way for the whole movement that became the mendicant friars, which was begun by a former canon regular, St. Dominic, and by St. Francis, a layman who may have become a deacon. St. Francis's initial movement was largely made up of lay brothers and gradually included priests. There were many small communities of men who followed the *Rule of St. Augustine,* and these gradually became the large order now known as the Augustinians. There are also Augustinian nuns (contemplative and cloistered) following the rule for women, but after the seventeenth century, communities of semicloistered nuns and active religious sisters also took up the *Rule of St. Augustine.* In days when habits indicated who belonged to what order, the black leather belt was usually a sign of someone who followed a version of the *Rule of St. Augustine.* Since medieval times the main body of Augustinian religious men have been called "friars" or "hermits." There are literally tens of thousands of Catholic religious men and women in the world today who follow the *Rule of St. Augustine* and even a small number of Anglican, Lutheran, and other Protestant religious who do.

Since St. Augustine was the dominant theologian in the Western church from the fifth century to the end of the thirteenth century, and still has a profound influence, it would not be difficult (but beyond the scope of this book) to access the effect of Augustine's thought and insights on the spiritualities of such great Christians as St. Benedict and the whole army of Benedictine saints and heroes, although they have a rule of their own. The same might be said for St. Francis and his followers, especially St. Bonaventure and St. Anthony. Augustine's influence on people as different as St. Ignatius Loyola and St. Teresa of Avila could be explored. The same could be said for people of modern times, such as Cardinal Newman, Romano Guardini, Cardinal de Lubac, and even the recent popes.

There are several excellent studies of St. Augustine's spirituality and its impact on religious life. I would recommend especially *Augustine's Ideal of the Religious Life*, by Adolar Zumkeller, O.S.A.,[1] and *Religious Life According to St. Augustine*, by Athanase Sage, A.A.[2] The more popular *If Augustine Were Alive*, by Theodore Tack, O.S.A., former general of the Augustinian friars, can be read with much benefit.[3] For those specifically interested in the rule, *Augustine of Hippo and His Monastic Rule*, by Fr. George Lawless, O.S.A., is highly recommended.[4]

The *Rule* itself is a little gem, establishing a religious life of charity, compassion, and frugality. Augustine was a strong advocate of poverty and penance and especially of fasting and simplicity of life. He was deeply disturbed when he discovered one of the brothers had secretly maintained ownership of a farm.[5] As already mentioned, he had troubles at the end of his life with dissent among his monks. The nuns he had founded with his sister disbanded. Sad to say, these difficulties have been typical of the experiences of founders of religious communities. Usually these founders have done what Augustine had suggested in the following passage from his *Rule*:[6]

Let there be no quarrels among you or, if they arise, end them as quickly as possible, lest your anger grow into hatred and the splinter become a beam (Mt 7:3-5) and make your heart a murderer's den. For we read in the Scriptures: "Whoever hates his brother is a murderer" (1 Jn 3:15).

Whoever has offended another by harshly reproaching, insulting, or calumniating him should be quick to make amends and he who was offended should forgive without reproaches. If, however, the injury has been mutual, both must forgive each other's trespasses (Mt. 6:12). And this on account of your prayers, which should be recited with greater sincerity each time you repeat them. He who is quick- tempered yet prompt to ask pardon from one he admittedly offended is better than the one who, although less inclined to anger, finds asking for forgiveness too difficult. He who is never willing to ask pardon or who from his heart does not do so (Mt. 18:35) has no purpose in being in a religious community even though he is not expelled. Take care then to avoid being too harsh in your words; but if they should escape your lips, let those same lips which caused the wound not be ashamed to speak the healing word.

We see from this passage that the realism and psychological insight of St. Augustine are all the more apparent in his approach to religious life. It is significant, I think, that although his little community of the Servants of God in Hippo did not survive, his insights into human nature with all its weaknesses and great possibilities have endured through the ages and given birth to so many religious communities.

Augustine on Women

Among many mistaken ideas about St. Augustine, those related to his attitude toward women are particularly troublesome. He is often pictured as hostile to women and as the source of much theological downgrading of women. This false evaluation is similar to the popular misconceptions about his teaching on sexuality, which we have already discussed.

Let us briefly look at his teaching in relation to the popular theological views and social attitudes of his time. To judge Augustine's views (or those of any ancient writer for that matter) by comparison with the accepted social attitudes of the Western industrialized nations of our day is not only unfair, it is just plain stupid. Augustine's views on the role of women and his personal relationship with women show him to be, in a single phrase, ahead of his time.

First, we see this in his profound love and respect for his mother, whom he so powerfully praises in the *Confessions* (see book 9) and with whom he shared his early intellectual examination of the Christian life and philosophy. Contrary to the custom of the time when women did not get involved in intellectual matters, Monica was a key participant in the dialogues at Cassiciacum.[7]

The pagan writers would never have been able to understand Augustine's regard and evidenced concern for his concubine. Her departure left him "cut and wounded."[8] We have seen that later on, as bishop, he was much concerned about the rights of married women in his own congregation—a concern that echoes his description of the treatment of wives in the *Confessions*.[9]

What is far more important in St. Augustine's teaching on women sharing equality with men is the *imago Dei,* the divine image. Kari Elisabeth Børresen, a Norwegian feminist scholar, in a very illuminating article points out that all the contemporary biblical strategies for establishing the equality of women with men as beings created in the image of God come from St. Augustine.[10] She states, "Augustine is the first author who directly confronts 1 Cor. 11, 7 by affirming that women are created in God's image." In the *Literal Meaning of Genesis,* Augustine writes: "A woman, for all her physical qualities as a woman is actually renewed in the spirit of her mind in the knowledge of God according to the image of her creator, and therein there is no male or female. . . . by the same token in the original creation of man, inasmuch as woman was a human being, she certainly had a mind, and a rational mind, and therefore she was also made in the image of God."[11]

It will come as a shock to the critics of Augustine (and probably to a lot of other people too), that the great bishop could even speak of the divine being in feminine terms. Mary Clark cites the following from the article "Augustine's View of Women," by the well-known Augustinian scholar T. J. Van Bavel:[12]

> The Psalmist made God father; he made God also mother. God is father because he created, because he calls, because he commands, because he governs. God is mother because God cherishes, because God nourishes, because God suckles, because God embraces (EnP 26.18).

Sister Clark also points out that Augustine championed the moral superiority of women over men. She writes:

> He was struck by the strength of faith in the great women martyrs of the first centuries and also by the virtue of ordinary Christian women who could serve as models and teachers for men. "Many husbands are surpassed by their wives; wives remain chaste, and men to not even want to be chaste" (S 9;280). Augustine dismissed the "double standard" and urged "Christian women not to show patience with their adulterous husbands and not to remain indifferent to such a situation" (S 292). One of the first to take up the cause of discrimination against women, Augustine spoke out against the Roman law which punished women for adultery while the men went free (S 153; 392). He also opposed the Roman law which allowed remarriage while both spouses lived (DNu II.8.7; S 9).[13]

Those seriously interested in correcting the very false impression that remains about Augustine's attitudes toward women, as well as his teachings on marriage, would do well to review them and many other questions in Sr. Clark's brief but comprehensive review of St. Augustine. While the word has many different connotations, Børresen does not hesitate to call St. Augustine's dramatic departure from the thinking of his time "feminist."[14]

Suggested Reading

Because of the introductory purposes of this book, I suggest the following reading program instead of a simple bibliography.

To Begin

Get a taste of St. Augustine. I suggest the following:

Rotelle, John, O.S.A. (ed.). *Augustine Day by Day*. Minute Meditations for Every Day. New York: Catholic Book Publishing Company, 1986.

Sheed, Frank. *Our Hearts Are Restless: The Prayer of St. Augustine*. New York: Crossroad, 1976.

Van Bavel, T. J., O.S.A. *Christians in the World*. New York: Catholic Book Publishing Company, 1980.

Read a biography. I suggest:

Brown, Peter. *Augustine of Hippo*. Berkeley and Los Angeles: University of California Press, 1969.

Read a good summary of Augustine's teachings:

Bourke, Vernon J. (ed.). *The Essential Augustine*. Indianapolis: Hackett Publishing Company, 1985.

Clark, Mary T., R.S.C.J., *Augustine*. Washington: Georgetown University Press, 1994.

John Paul II. *Augustine of Hippo—Apostolic Letter*. Boston: St. Paul Editions, 1986.

O'Meara, John J. (ed.) *An Augustine Reader*. New York: Doubleday, 1973.

Read the *Confessions.*

A variety of contemporary translations are available. Pusey's old translation is difficult to read. I prefer Frank Sheed's translation, now published by Hackett Books, Boston. Introduction by Peter Brown.

The Confessions of St. Augustine. Trans. E. B. Pusey. Introduction by Fulton J. Sheen. New York: Modern Library (Random House), 1949.

Confessions of St. Augustine. Trans. F. J. Sheed. New York: Sheed & Ward, 1943. Now available from Hackett Books, Boston, with introduction by Peter Brown.

Further Reading

Second Level:

Augustine. *The City of God* (abridged). Introduction by Etienne Gilson. Translated by Walsh, Zema, Monahan, and Honan. New York: Doubleday Image Book, 1958.

———. *Sermons.* Translated by Edmund Hill, O.P. Brooklyn: New City Press.

———. *The Trinity.* Translated by Edmund Hill, O.P. Brooklyn: New City Press, 1990.

Clark, Mary (ed.). *Augustine of Hippo.* Classics of Western Spirituality. New York: Paulist Press, 1984.

Przywara, Eric, S.J. (ed.). *The Augustine Synthesis.* New York: Sheed & Ward, 1949.

Various volumes from Fathers of the Church series and Ancient Christian Writers series.

Third Level:

The following suggestions will open up a vast bibliography of studies on St. Augustine.

Augustinian Heritage Institute. *Augustinian Studies.* Villanova, PA: Villanova University.

Gilson, Etienne. *The Christian Philosophy of St. Augustine.* New York: Random House, 1960. Now available through Octagon-Hippocrene Books, New York.

Notes

Introduction

1. *The Confessions of St. Augustine*. London: Medici Society, 1930.
2. *Confessions of St. Augustine*. Trans. F. J. Sheed (New York: Sheed and Ward, 1944). In this book all further citations of the *Confessions* are from Sheed's translation unless specifically noted.
3. Classics of Western Spirituality (New York: Paulist Press, 1984).
4. *The Works of St. Augustine* (Brooklyn, NY: New City Press, 1991).
5. Ibid., vol. 3, *Sermons*, 198.
6. *Confessions* 4.4.
7. Peter Brown, *Augustine of Hippo* (London: Faber & Faber, 1967), 390.
8. Ibid., 248.
9. Ibid.
10. Ibid., 138.

Chapter One
The Young Augustine—The *Confessions*

1. *Ep.* 231.6. Quoted from Peter Brown, *Augustine of Hippo*, 427.
2. Angelo Berardino, ed., *Patrology IV*, trans. Placid Solari (Westminister, Md.: Christian Classics, 1991), 343.
3. Brown, *Augustine*, 160.
4. *Retractions* 2.43; quoted from Brown, *Augustine*, 430.
5. Romano Guardini, *The Conversion of Augustine* (Westminister, Md.: Newman Press, 1960), 17.

Chapter Two
Augustine the Philosopher

1. Vernon J. Bourke, *The Essential Augustine* (Indianapolis: Hackett Publishing Co., 1985), 19–27.
2. Ibid., 19.
3. Ibid., 20.
4. E. Przywara, ed., *Augustine Synthesis* (New York: Sheed & Ward, 1945), 39 (adapted by the author).
5. Gilson, E., *The Christian Philosophy of St. Augustine* (New York:

Random House, 1960), 3–44. This volume is also now available through Octagon-Hippocrene Books, New York.

6. Przywara, ed., *Augustine Synthesis,* 29. Trans. E. B. Pusey (adapted by the author).

7. John J. O'Meara, *An Augustine Reader* (New York: Doubleday Image Books, 1973), 34.

8. Ibid., 37.

9. Ibid., 38–41. Trans. R. E. Cleveland (London, 1910) (adapted by the author).

10. Bourke, *Essential Augustine,* 257.

11. Ibid., 37.

12. Ibid., 36. Trans. M. Dods (Edinburgh: T. Clarke, 1871), 7. 405.

13. Adapted by the author. Cf. Przywara, ed., *Augustine Synthesis,* 14.

14. Przywara, ed., *Augustine Synthesis,* 16 (adapted by the author).

15. Ibid., 358 (adapted by the author).

16. Ibid., 358 (adapted by the author).

17. Ibid., 357 (adapted by the author).

18. Gareth B. Matthews, "The Inner Man," in *Augustine: A Collection of Critical Essays,* ed. R. A. Markus (New York: Doubleday Anchor Books, 1972), 177.

19. Cited from Matthews, "The Inner Man," 177.

20. See Brown, *Augustine,* chaps. 30 and 33; Gilson, *Christian Philosophy,* 127ff.; John M. Rist, "Augustine on Free Will and Predestination," in *Augustine,* ed. Markus, 218–52.

21. Rist, "Augustine on Free Will," 220.

22. Ibid.

23. Augustine, *City of God,* book 5, ed. Vernon J. Bourke (New York: Doubleday Image Books, 1958) 98–118.

24. *Enchirideon ad Laurentiam* 31.117; cf. Rist, "Augustine on Free Will," 223.

25. Rist, "Augustine on Free Will," 222–23.

26. Cited from Przywara, ed., *Augustine Synthesis,* 125 (adapted by the author).

27. Ibid. (adapted by the author).

28. Brown, *Augustine,* 432.

29. Ibid., 406.

30. *St. Augustine on the Psalms,* trans. S. Hebgin and F. Corrigan (Ancient Christian Writers; Westminster, Md.: Newman Press, 1961), 2. 274–75.

Chapter Three
Augustine—The Preacher of the Word

1. Pp. 249–56.

2. All citations from the *Liturgy of the Hours* (Office of Readings) are

taken from the Catholic Book Publishing Edition (New York, 1975). Translations are by the International Committee on English in the Liturgy. Vol. 1, p. 379.

3. *Liturgy of the Hours*, 1. 527.

4. Augustine, *Sermons for Christmas and Epiphany,* trans. Thomas C. Lawler (Ancient Christian Writers; Westminster, Md.: Newman Press, 1952), 71–72. (Now Paulist Press, Ramsey, N.J.)

5. *Liturgy of the Hours*, 3. 1813–15.

6. Clark, *Augustine of Hippo*, 199–201.

7. Bernard McGinn, *The Foundations of Mysticism* (New York: Crossroad, 1991), 249.

8. Ibid., 250.

9. *Liturgy of the Hours*, 2. 366.

10. Ibid., 2. 168–70.

11. Leon Bloy, *The Pilgrim of the Absolute* (New York: Pantheon Books, 1947), 275.

12. *Liturgy of the Hours*, 4. 102.

13. Ibid., 2. 920.

14. Ibid., 4. 534.

15. St. Augustine, *Homily XLIII on the Gospel of St. John* (A Select Library of the Nicene and Post-Nicene Fathers, ed. P. Schaff; Grand Rapids, Mich.: Eerdmans, 1956), 7. 241.

Chapter Four
Augustine—The Mystic

1. Dom Cuthbert Butler, O.S.B., *Western Mysticism* (2d ed.; London: Constable Publishers, 1926), 20. The entire chapter should be read. I am indebted to Dom Cuthbert in these pages.

2. Bernard McGinn, *The Foundations of Mysticism*, 252f. This superb article should be read when you are ready. I also express my indebtedness to Dr. McGinn.

3. Ibid., 252.

4. See introduction, n. 3.

5. Dom Cuthbert Butler, O.S.B., *Western Mysticism* (New York: Dutton, 1923), 21.

6. Cited from ibid., 21.

7. Ibid.

8. Ibid., 24–25.

9. Ibid., 21.

10. Ibid.

11. Ibid., 25.

12. Ibid., 22.

13. Benedict J. Groeschel, *Spiritual Passages* (New York, Crossroad, 1989), chaps. 6 and 7.

14. McGinn, *Foundations,* 239.

15. Butler, *Western Mysticism,* 22–23.

16. Ibid., 23–24.

17. See N. Heler, *The Exemplar,* trans. Sr. Ann Edward (2 vols.; Chicago: Priory Press, 1962).

18. Cf. Augustine, *Literal Meaning of Genesis,* trans. H. Taylor (Ancient Christian Writers 42; New York: Newman Press, 1982).

19. Bourke, *Essential Augustine,* 126.

20. McGinn, *Foundations,* 235.

21. Ibid.

22. Bonaventure, *The Soul's Journey into God,* ed. E. Cousins (Classics of Western Spirituality; New York: Paulist Press, 1978), 113.

23. Clark, *Augustine,* 365.

24. McGinn, *Foundations,* 242–43.

25. Butler, *Western Mysticism,* 45.

26. Ibid., 23.

27. From John E. Rotelle, O.S.A., ed., *We Are Your Servants,* trans. Audrey Fellows (Philadelphia: Augustinian Press, 1986).

28. Brown, *Augustine,* 409.

29. Butler, *Western Mysticism,* 20.

30. Cited from Rotelle, ed., *We Are Your Servants,* 101–3.

Chapter Five
Augustine—Theologian of the Trinity

1. Edmund Hill gives a fine review of Augustine's patristic sources as well as his scriptural basis (*The Works of St. Augustine* [Brooklyn: New City Press, 1991], 27–45).

2. J. H. Newman, *The Arians* (London: Basil, Montague & Pickering, 1876).

3. Clark, *Augustine,* xvi.

4. McGinn, *Foundations,* 247.

5. Hill, *The Works of St. Augustine, The Trinity,* 25.

6. Ibid.

7. I must mention that I do not always agree with Fr. Hill's application of Augustine to the contemporary theological battlefields, but he makes his points well. Two instances of my disagreement are the following: his use of the Anglican bishop John A. T. Robinson's book *Honest to God* at the end of the introduction (p. 56). At a delightful tea with the Bishop and Mrs. Robinson over Devonshire cream and rhubarb marmalade in their home on the Sussex Downs (hollyhocks, Irish setter, and all), I heard Dr. Robinson clearly distance himself both from this book and the theological currents that it set off. He assured me that *Honest to God* was

the result of a depression caused by a slipped disc in his back. I also think that Fr. Hill's dismissal of the significance of the words *persona* in Latin and *hypostasis* in Greek for the persons of the Trinity needs a lot of qualification. Obviously these terms applied to the Trinity are analogues, as is anything we say about God, but the usefulness of these analogues is born out by this entire book on the Trinity and, in fact, by the whole theological understanding of Christianity. Why pick this one word out for attack, especially since this one word is of such great importance in contemporary psychology and might even lead us out of some of the abysmal confusion at the present time about the divine person of Christ? I refer to the Jesus-with-identity-crisis school of thought that makes up the party of modern *agnotes* (if you are not familiar with this term, in the ancient church it meant people who denied that Christ knew the day of judgment). I think Fr. Hill's use of Raimundo Pannikkar's cynical remark to some African bishops suggesting that they were fortunate not to have words in their native language for "nature" and "person" is disconcerting. I know a number of African bishops who would agree with me. These difficulties do not keep Fr. Hill's work from being a marvelous map for exploring Augustine's great work.

8. Hill, *The Works of St. Augustine*, 66–67.

9. *Sermons* 130, 9, and 17. Cf. Hill, *The Works of St. Augustine*, 239–40. Fr. Hill discusses the difficulty many will have when reading what he calls the Platonic style of discourse. His explanation may be some help to those who do not think this way. My personal opinion is that there are many who do think this way, including me.

10. Cited from Clark, *Augustine*, 314–15.

11. Benedict J. Groeschel, *A Still Small Voice: The Church's Teaching on Reported Private Revelations* (San Francisco: Ignatius Press, 1992).

12. Cited from Clark, *Augustine*, 326.

13. Ibid., 312.

14. John Henry Newman, *The Idea of a University* (London: Longmans Green, 1901), 217–18.

Chapter Six
Augustine the Historian—The City of God

1. Gilson, *The Christian Philosophy*, 21–25.

2. *City of God*, ed. Bourke (see chap. 2, n. 3), 10. All references to the *City of God* in this chapter are to this edition.

3. *The Literal Meaning of Genesis.*

4. Cited from Rotelle, ed., *We Are Your Servants*, 35.

5. *City of God* 19.14.

6. Ibid.

7. Ibid., 19.19.
8. Ibid.
9. Ibid., 450–51.
10. See Brown, *Augustine*, 432.

Chapter Seven
Augustine as a Spiritual Guide

1. From Augustine, *The Moral Behavior of the Catholic Church,* in Bourke, ed., *Essential Augustine,* 157–59. Translation of *The Works of Aurelius Augustinus,* ed. Marcus Dods (Edinburgh: Clark, 1871) (adapted by the author).

2. *Letter* 130. From *Liturgy of the Hours,* trans. International Committee on English in the Liturgy, 4. 407.

3. Rotelle, ed., *We Are Your Servants,* 138–40.

4. Hill, ed., *Sermons,* vol. 3 of *The Works of St. Augustine,* 454, 455.

5. F. Van Der Meer, *Augustine the Bishop* (London/New York: Sheed & Ward, 1961), 78–110.

6. Cited from Clark, *Augustine,* 232.

7. Ibid., 250.

8. *Opera omnia S. Augustin,* vol. 2 (Patrologia Latina; Paris: Migne, 1841), 1027–29.

Addenda

1. Trans. Edmund Colledge, O.S.A. New York: Fordham University Press, 1986.

2. Ed. John Rotelle, O.S.A. Brooklyn: New City Press, 1990.

3. New York: Alba House, 1989.

4. Oxford: Clarendon Press, 1987.

5. Brown, *Augustine,* 410.

6. Clark, *Augustine,* 491–92.

7. Brown, *Augustine,* 118ff. Also the chapter on Monica (pp. 28ff.).

8. *Confessions,* 4.4.

9. Ibid., 9.9.

10. "Patristic 'Feminism': The Case of Augustine," *Augustine Studies* 25 (1994): 139–52.

11. Cf. *The Literal Meaning of Genesis,* op. cit., 1.99.

12. *Augustine* (Washington, D.C.: Georgetown University Press, 1994) 127.

13. Ibid.

14. Clark, *Augustine,* 144ff.